CHILDREN AT RISK

NETWORKS IN ACTION

DEDICATION

To he who adopted me, aged twelve, into his family. To the greatest Dad any orphan can ever wish for. To the Father of the fatherless, God: the King of glory, the Lord of lords.

A father to the fatherless . . . is God in his holy dwelling. (Psalm 68:5)

Children at Risk

Networks in Action

PATRICK MCDONALD

WITH EMMA GARROW

World Vision International
800 West Chestnut Avenue, Monrovia, CA 91016-3198, USA

ISBN 1-887983-22-8

MARC books are published by World Vision International, 800 W. Chestnut Avenue, Monrovia, California 91016-3198, U.S.A.

Printed in the United States of America. Cover design and typesetting: Richard Sears. Cover Photo: Jon Warren/World Vision.

All Scripture quotations, unless otherwise indicated, are from the New International Version © 1973, 1978, 1984 by the International Bible Society.

This book was originally published in the United Kingdom as *Reaching Children in Need*.

All the stories of children mentioned in this book are true, but names and places may have been changed in the interests of child protection.

Contents

Acknowledgements

The task of writing a book is far more elaborate than initially antici-pated. It takes a lot of work and involves a lot of time and people. This book is no different. Yet it was the Lord who first prompted me to write this book as I walked along the Thames near Port Meadow in Oxford one autumn day. Words would never suffice to describe my gratitude for his work in my life. To him is due any honour and glory.

The vision for this book really started in 1991 in Santa Cruz, Bolivia, where Roger Hulford introduced me to the children of the streets. His brother, David Hulford, was an equally important mentor during my time there. Since then a multitude of people have given generously of their time and energy in taking me around childcare projects, in wel-coming me to their offices and in pouring me endless cups of tea and coffee.

Martin Hull was the first to join me officially in the task of writing this book and helped me to formulate the initial outline. Susan Cuthbert later helped to condense and edit the initial content and proved in-valuable in so many ways, as did Steven Gertz and Sarah O'Connor, who checked the detail on stories, verified statistics and in so many other ways made this book a reality. My very special thanks to them and to Emma Garrow, whose critical role as shadow writer in many ways made this book what it is.

My thanks go to Katharine Miles, Ian de Villiers, Neil Cuthbert, Emma Randall, Glenn Miles, Charity and David Scott, Doug and Janna McConnell, Ernie Addicott, Michael Pollitt, Ross Wilson, Victoria Warwick, Sally Clarke, Wendy Strachan, Stephen Tollestrup, Tony Senewiratne, Tom Houston, Paul Stephenson, Dan Brewster, Stanley Davies, Raymond Samuel, Josephina Guitterrez, Barry Slauenwhite, Lucy Palma, Carolyn Owen, Chris Jackson, Richard Herkes, Clive Calver, Baroness Cox, Steve Chalke, Doug Nichols, Francis Sunderaraj, David Howard, Bryant Myers, Nola Leach, Wes Stafford and Charie Fibbs, who all gave helpful comments.

Finally, thank you to the heroes of my world: the Christian networkers who by their service daily seek to connect and empower the Christian community of outreach to children in need. I am married to one of the most good looking, Emily, and stand in debt to her, to the rest of the staff at Viva Network and to others who around the world work to facilitate networking and partnerships for this vital ministry.

Oxford, England
October 1999

Foreword

I first became aware of this remarkable story in 1995, about 18 months after Viva Network began.

Patrick McDonald came to me to ask how we could link him and Viva Network with the Lausanne Committee for World Evangelization. Being approached by an organization that was not yet two years old was unusual. Of course, I looked for its track record. I was astonished at what had been done in such a short time. Few organizations become international so rapidly. Patrick was already talking about Viva Network being in 14 countries. He also seemed to be in touch with all the people he needed to contact, given the nature of the network.

Patrick was no maverick striking out on his own, regardless of those with a much longer record of working with children in need than he and his friends had. He was taking great pains to talk to and learn from both the big organizations and the grass-roots Christian workers. He has maintained that stance with great patience and persistence and is earning the respect and trust of veterans in this kind of work.

It has been fascinating to watch the growth of Viva Network. It has not only spread geographically, but it has progressively covered the issues that inevitably arise when you turn your attention to children in need.

You will find several strands in this book. There is a cumulative series of almost terrifying statistics. Heart-warming and heart-wrenching stories about real children in need tumble over each other. It sounds a constant plea that the people of God should do more about them and do it together.

The sense of the millstone hanging round the neck of those who put stumbling-blocks in the way of the children is never far away. Yet there is also the happy laughter of children who were lost but have been found and are at home somewhere at last.

It is a book to read, mark, learn and inwardly digest — and buy another for a caring friend — to network with.

Tom Houston
Oxford, August 1999

Time to Arise   *1*

Arise, cry out in the night, as the watches of the night begin;
pour out your heart like water in the presence of the Lord.
Lift up your hands to him for the lives of your children, who
faint from hunger at the head of every street.
(Lamentations 2:19)

It is two o'clock in the morning in Bogota, Colombia, and nine-year-old Jarislon shudders from the cold as he tries to lay aside his fears and get some sleep. As he huddles beneath a shop awning, he is haunted by the questions that crowd his mind: 'Will I be alive in the morning? How will death come? Will it hurt? Or will it be so sudden that I won't even feel it?'

But when he thinks back over his short life, he feels that even nights like these are preferable to what he has left behind. Jarislon has run away from a shack of a home and a mother unable to feed her children on anything much other than her own rage. He knows the shock of a hard wall against his head, a sharp foot in his side, and the terrible sight of his mother crouching, sobbing that she wished she were dead. Alone now, struggling to hold onto the newspapers that were supposed to protect him from the wind and rain, Jarislon has some sympathy with his mother. The cold up here in the Andes is piercing and the sweater he had rescued from a rubbish bin has been stolen by some older boys. He wishes he had a dad to protect him. But then he remembers the succession of men his mother brought home, one of whom could have been his dad, but then again, maybe not. Thinking of them, Jarislon's young heart fills with hatred. He pulls the newspapers up to his chin again and concentrates on surviving till morning.

ᕦ ᕤ ᕦ

Meanwhile, it is seven o'clock on a chilly, misty morning in Oxford, England, and a group of students and other young people meet to pray. Some bleary-eyed from their early start, others fresh-cheeked from their cycle rides to this college flat near Magdalen Bridge, they gather round a small gas fire with mugs of tea or coffee in their hands and share their experiences of working with children in Latin America. They close their eyes and begin to pray. Many of them know about the hardships faced by children on the streets every day. They know about the hard work and sacrifice put in by committed Christian childcare workers, and they know that often it is just not enough to help the children. Now returned to Oxford, to their studies and their work, they cannot forget what they have seen, nor fail to turn to God in tearful prayer together. Believing in a God who can solve the most mighty problems, they also believe that it is him who keeps them there on their knees in fervent hope that he will use even them to change the situation. And in the chill of that morning, it is God who warms their hearts with his presence and his direction.

ᔦ ᔦ ᔦ

Half-past noon on the same day in Vellore, India, and Pastor Damaraj breaks the news to the dozen children who call him 'Uncle' over their meagre rice lunch. All attempts to raise money for the Christian Light Children's Home have failed and the children must all go back to where they came from. Pastor Damaraj's heart breaks as he watches the young faces of his charges take in what is happening. He longs for a way for them to continue the education they have been able to re-ceive while living with him. Pastor Damaraj can tell that the young-est, Kanda, is trying hard to hold back his tears. After four years in the home, Kanda will now have to go back to his village in the hills, the remote home of members of the Adivasi tribe. Kanda's brother and sister fell ill and died while very young as no doctors ever make the trek to Kanda's village, and his parents had no money to go down into the town to buy medicine. There is no school in the village and Kanda will not be able to continue his learning.

But there is nothing Pastor Damaraj can do. Today is the cook's last day and there is no more money even to buy food for tomorrow. The home must close.

Children in need

These are true life events, though the names have been changed. Jarislon spent that night and many others on the streets. Pastor Damaraj did close his children's home. In the autumn of 1994, a group of young adults did begin to meet regularly on Monday mornings in Oxford to pray for children in need and Christian childcare workers around the world. Many of them had seen the needs, met the kids and been behind the soup pot, serving with a ladle in the many project sites on the streets of our cities the world over. They knew that stories such as Jarislon's and Pastor Damaraj's were true for a multitude of other children and childcare workers as well. For them the term 'children in need' was not jargon. They knew some of those children and they wanted to help them.

Who are children in need? Surprisingly, there is as yet no agreed terminology to define them. To my mind they are children who need help. Pure and simple. It could be easy for Christians to make a case for identifying every child as in need or 'at risk' — the spiritual risk of growing up without God. A friend and colleague of mine in the Christian childcare community, Glenn Miles, defines children at risk as 'children in danger of not reaching their God-given potential, physically, environmentally, mentally, socially and spiritually'. He is the first to point out that his definition includes all children.

However, in our pursuit to define a child in need we must be more specific. Tony Senewiratne, an outstanding children's project leader in Sri Lanka, offers this definition: 'Children deprived of the normal benefits of love and care which would create healthy development, immaterial of the further privilege of material luxuries.'

The American psychologist, Abraham H. Maslow (1908–70), developed the idea of a 'hierarchy of needs'. This sequential list starts with physiological needs — food, water, absence of pain — then moves on to safety, a sense of belonging, self-esteem, and a sense of identity, before ending with our aesthetic needs to be creative and to nurture a sense of wonder. Violinist, Isaac Stern, summarizes Maslow's hierarchy of need well when he states: 'Every child has the right to know that there is beauty in the world.'

It is on the concept of our 'rights' that most secular child development agencies base their definitions of children in need, using the UN convention on the rights of the child. While this is another useful tool, it nonetheless neglects the most basic right of any child: the right and need to know their Creator. The 'Oxford Statement on Children at Risk' puts it well when it says: 'We affirm that all children are at risk from the very moment of their conception...However, it is for the neglected and exploited children of our generation that our hearts cry out.'

I was one of those young adults who met in Oxford to pray back in 1994 and I want to tell you about children who need our help; children who suffer in the worst imaginable ways, those whom no one loves and for whom love and human comfort are strange, unknown quantities they have never experienced. I also want to tell you about what is happening to lessen their plight; and about what can still be done.

I often talk about these children because I have come to know so many of them, to love them and care for them and to deeply respect their struggle for life and hope. Someone once said that the longest journey of the human experience is the 18 inches from the mind to the heart and I believe that that is true. In the course of this book you will read mind-numbing statistics about children who are more than at risk — they have already been violated. The figures you will see before you will no doubt be too large to take in; the problems they represent too huge to contemplate.

Whenever that happens, go back and remember Jarislon in Bogota. For unless you understand something of what it means to be a child who is homeless, abandoned, neglected and hungry, what you read in the following pages will make no difference in your heart or mind and subsequently no difference at all to the children in your city, your country, your world.

I want to tell you about the response of God's amazing people, the Christian family, which, despite all its flaws and shortcomings, is responding like no other group of people to the needs of children at risk. Conservative estimates suggest the existence of more than 25,000 projects, staffed by over 100,000 full-time workers, reaching in excess of 2 million children on a daily basis.

I hope to share with you some of my findings about the nature and status of that segment of Christian work, as well as some of the strategies that have emerged through the network of groups increasingly known as the Viva Network. I would like to talk about the importance of making children in need a key priority for the church and her mission as we move into the twenty-first century, and about how networking can help her to do that. All too often ministries to children in need are isolated and unrecognized, cut off from like-minded people or potential helpers. Like Pastor Damaraj, their staff have difficulty in accomplishing all that they set out to do, since time, support, money and resources are all limited. They themselves are weary and are crying out for help.

Yet there is hope. I often go for walks with an old missionary who for many years served in Africa. He constantly reminds me that a point of view is only a view from a point. If we want to understand God's point of view, we need to wear his glasses. Let us try to imagine the heart and mind of God. We are the Lord's ambassadors, agents and advocates, and are part of the most powerful movement in the world today: the Christian church. It is not just that we must clench our fists and close our eyes tight and somehow the needs of children and their carers will be met. If we grasp the need and understand that an almighty God has a solution to this enormous problem, we will find ways to counteract it effectively. God has an answer.

As we prayed on those Monday mornings, we were overwhelmed by the challenge that presented itself to us: this challenge to serve the needs of children and their carers. All we really had was God's clear word to us to go and his promise to go with us. We did not have a vision statement, an introductory leaflet, a bank account or legal status. We were certainly out of our depth, but we were hungry to learn and excited about the prospect of embarking upon a venture long overdue.

God has always called his people to take hold of his standards and his goals. As we rise to this we will realize the greatness of his provision. The missionary to China, J. Hudson Taylor, said: 'Depend on it, God's work done in God's way will never lack God's supplies.' This is a time of big problems, but also of big solutions.

Prayer from Mexico

I am only a spark —
Make me a fire.

I am only a string —
Make me a lyre.

I am only a drop —
Make me a fountain.

I am only an anthill —
Make me a mountain.

I am only a feather —
Make me a wing.

I am only a rag —
Make me a king!

A Generation Lost   2

*Therefore go and make disciples of all nations, baptising
them in the name of the Father and of the Son and of the
Holy Spirit, and teaching them to obey everything I have
commanded you. (Matthew 28:19–20)*

On a visit to Cape Town in 1997 I met a street child named Kevin. His
clothes were in rags, his hair was crawling with lice, and he stank in
the most unceremonious way of goodness knows what. As we chat-
ted for some time it became obvious that Kevin was somewhere else,
far away on a cloud of glue thinner. It occurred to me that rather than
conduct mere small talk it would be better to ask him a direct question. I proceeded in the same casual way as before but asked him,
'Kevin, what is your innermost desire?'

He paused, as though struck by something, and with a rare clarity of mind
fixed his eyes on mine and answered, 'To honour the Lord my God.'

I reeled with the impact of his answer. As music blared from a nearby
disco I tried to follow this new line of conversation. ' Where do you
want to start?' I asked him.

He thought for a time and replied, 'I must bring my family together.
My brother is in a children's home, my sister in another, my father is
dead and I don't know where my mother is.'

ℛ ℛ ℛ

Children and childhood are at risk as never before. At the turn of this
millennium almost one-third of the world's population are under the
age of 15; that is 1.8 billion children.[1] Of all children born today 80 per
cent live in developing countries in Asia, Africa and Latin America
and some parts of Europe where extreme poverty is prevalent.[2] In fact,

---

[1] Global Evangelization Movement website: http://www.gem- werc.org/index.htm

[2] *Relay,* second quarter, 1998, as quoted in *Statistics Concerning the Needs of Under-
privileged and Street Children Worldwide,* October 1998 (Street Children Ministries).

the horror of childhood destroyed and damaged is increasingly prevalent in almost every country, context and culture across the globe.

What is more, it is anticipated that between 1998 and 2025, 4.5 billion
children will be born.[3] As 97 per cent of world population growth takes
place in the developing world,[4] multitudes of children will endure a
life of high social risk. UNICEF states that 130 million primary school
age children have no access to education[5] and therefore no means by
which to pull themselves up out of the quagmire of poverty and give
their own children a better chance.

Yet behind each of the vast numbers and overwhelming statistics hides
a face, a name, a life and a soul, like Kevin and his lost brother and
sister, seeking to be welcomed, to be part of a safe environment, to be
loved and to have the freedom to dream the great dreams of childhood. Life as God intended was meant to be more than mere survival,
but a life full and rich in exploration, adventure and fulfilment.

The homeless

I used to work with children on the streets of Santa Cruz in Bolivia. I
made many friends there. My Spanish was not good so I was limited
to playing rugby, giving swings and generally keeping a bunch of street
kids out of trouble. One of my friends was a girl, not yet 13 years of
age. She did not play too well as she had been abused badly. Forced to
work in a brothel, this child had already conceived three times and
had, due to the nature of her occupation, been forced to abort the
babies. So far as we knew, this had been done by repeated kicks to the
stomach.

Another child I got to know was Santos from San Salvador in Central
America. I met him one bright morning near Parque La Libertad (Park
of Freedom) and stopped to chat. We parted, but I came across him
three hours later, dying in the ruins of an old building. Santos, being

---

[3] World Population Profile 1998, Thomas McDewitt, International Program Center,
    US Census Bureau 1999, website.

[4] Ibid.

[5] *The State of the World's Children 1999:* Education, UNICEF, as quoted from Facts &
    Figures 1998 (New York: UNICEF).

hungry, had stolen an apple from a street stall and been chased by the police, who eventually caught him with a machete and accidentally slit his stomach open, literally, from side to side. The anxious policemen had panicked, and gathering what they could had lifted Santos into the old building nearby where I found him a few hours later.

More than any other type of child at risk, the street child has caught the imagination of the public. Headlines the world over have brought attention to the needs of these modern-day Oliver Twists. However, sociologically speaking, street children are just the tip of the proverbial iceberg. For every child you see on the streets, many more are at risk, albeit perhaps in slightly less visible situations.

Street children are not a new phenomenon. Children have lived and worked on the streets for generations. However, the scale of the problem is far greater than ever before. Given their transitory nature and the different terms used to define a street child, there is perpetual disagreement about the actual number of children on the streets at any one time, so reliable statistics are hard to come by. Nevertheless it can be said that somewhere between 100 and 200 million children worldwide are at least working, if not living, on the streets.[6]

The *Encyclopedia of World Problems and Human Potential* gives us some idea of the vastness of this problem when it casts a torch on the notorious Indian city of Calcutta. It says: 'The present day numbers of street children in single cities like Calcutta may be equal to the total population of those cities in the last century.'[7]

Children come to live or work on the streets for a variety of reasons. The bright lights of big cities draw families and individuals from the countryside in the hope of finding work, but the reality rarely matches the dreams and the impoverished families more often than not end up worse off than before. They send their children onto the streets to begin working, usually selling home-made goods or begging, to help the whole family to survive.

---

6   Robert Linthicum, 'Exploiting Children in Our Cities', *Together*, April–June 42:1994, as quoted in Phyllis Kilbourn (ed.), *Children in Crisis: A New Commitment* (Monrovia, USA: MARC, 1996).

7   *Encyclopedia of World Problems and Human Potential* (Union of International Associations 1994).

Or perhaps a child's home has disintegrated completely and the street is the only place to call home. Consider the story of Ramesh in India, who moved to a new region with his family so that his father could find work in the city. They set up home in a shanty town and Ramesh's father took casual work to feed his family of four. Depressed and discouraged, he took to spending his wages on drink and was eventually forced to borrow from a money-lender to pay the rent. The rate of interest was high and the family found it impossible to pay. One evening, just before the rains, the debt collectors came round. Ramesh's father was out and in despair his mother took her own life. Where could Ramesh and the remaining members of his family go now but to the streets?

Alternatively, children may find themselves on the streets simply because they are left there, abandoned by desperate parents. They may be orphaned or have run away from an unbearable home life, like Sasha in St Petersburg, whose stepfather beat him, leaving him with the scars to prove it. Winters in this northern and notoriously damp Russian city are beyond description, but if you had to choose between a knife at your throat and the searing cold of a winter's night on St Petersburg's streets, which would you choose? Fear is a great decider and one of the things that I find again and again in the children I get to know is the massive presence of fear. It is one thing to be scared by something for a moment; it is quite another to be continually frightened. It is one thing to wake up from a bad dream and allow the reason that comes with wakefulness to chase away what scared you in sleep; it is another to endure the dull persistent ache of fear.

A friend of mine, a Baptist pastor from Costa Rica, once started a shelter for street children in San Francisco de dos Rios near the capital of San Jose. He told me how he had come to understand the issue of fear in these children. When they came to his shelter, they were each given their own mattress and their own blanket and there in the safety of his little Baptist church the children slept peacefully and, mostly, for a very long time. Almost without fail, however, most of them would wet their mattresses on their first night in the church, as in the safety of shelter they finally relaxed. The fear and utter rejection most of these children suffer make it difficult for those like Sasha to get close to any adult who attempts to befriend them in the future.

Once on the streets anything could happen to a child. They may find rest each night in a doorway, a cardboard box or a sewer; they may find food and clothing by scavenging in other people's waste or by begging; they may even make a small income from shoe-shining or selling the discarded goods they find around the city. Often income is gained from theft or prostitution, though as a rule there tend to be more street boys than street girls. Girls are easier to absorb into an 'off-the-street environment', working either as maids, bar girls or prostitutes.

The streets of our world's cities are not safe places for children. Life there subjects them to violence. Crime syndicates often make use of them because they are easy to spare and missed by nobody should they disappear. Other children may end up in gangs, formed out of a need for protection but riddled with infighting and often just as dangerous as anything else a child on the streets might face. Gang leaders may demand a share of a member's daily earnings, while gangs made up of older boys may push younger children away from more lucrative patches of town. All street kids, whether in a gang or not, are in possible danger from paedophiles. Neither are the police necessarily their protectors, as my friend Santos well knew.

Life is so hard that in order to dull the feelings of hunger, cold and pain, many children take to glue sniffing or drugs. Of Latin America's 40 million street children,[8] half are estimated to be addicted to inhalants.[9] Brain damage and death often result from these addictions. Even when children are offered the opportunity of leaving the streets, the road to recovery can be long and cumbersome. Many children are warmed by the protection offered by Christian projects and are able to move forward into a better life. Others, like Jose in Honduras, find it hard to trust the security on offer to them.

Jose ran away from his home in Guatemala when he overheard his mother and her boyfriend talking about sending him out to work. With the help of an aunt, he made it to Honduras where the police picked

---

[8] Child Hope, as quoted in *Children at Risk: A global education curriculum series, Street Children* (The Office on Global Education (OGE), USA).

[9] *Growing Up on the Rough Side* (The Gospel Message 1998).

him up and took him to a Christian children's project. After a while, he ran away and was not heard of again. Street life can be addictive for a child for whom love and concern are strangers.

I have mentioned a few children by name, but if we were to say the name of every street child in the world, using a second per name, it would take us more than three years to reach 100 million. What hope is there for so many children whose lives are likely to end before they reach adulthood?

- In 1990 it was estimated that 20,000 children slept on New York's streets nightly.[10]

- In Bogota, Colombia, 85 per cent of all street children die before they turn 15.[11]

- Half of the beggars on UK streets spent their childhood in care and a quarter slept on the streets before they were 16.[12]

The war-torn

Ten-year-old Grace, her three sisters and her nine-year-old brother, Mugabi, lived in a village in Uganda with their mother, father and grandparents. Their family life was good, they received some education at a local school, and though they were poor, they were fairly contented. Then one day a band of rebel soldiers attacked their village. There was great panic among the villagers. Some tried to run away but were shot in the back for the attempt. Homes were burned down and women raped. Children were taken away. Grace and Mugabi were hurrying to a hiding place with their grandmother when a rebel shot her and dragged them off to join a group of other village children. The children were taken to a camp some miles away and there the boys and girls, some of them brothers and sisters and cousins, were separated. The boys were trained to become soldiers and to kill. The girls were kept as domestic helpers and substitute wives for the rebels who captured them. Grace and Mugabi rarely saw each other from that day

---

[10] Church World Service 1991, Global Calendar/New Internationalist (Philadelphia: New Society Publishers 1990).

[11] Action International Ministries.

[12] *IDEA,* magazine of the Evangelical Alliance in the UK, January 1995.

on and they never learned what happened to the rest of their family.

This may sound too incredible to be true. How can a village be peaceful one day and torn apart the next? How can children go to school, help their parents at home and play with each other one day, but be soldiers and concubines the next? Yet this is a reality for Graces and Mugabis all over Uganda and other war-torn parts of Africa.

Seren Boyd of (TEARFund) UK writes:

> A child captures a grown-up in the sights of his gun and slowly pulls the trigger. This is no water pistol and this is no game. Someone has fallen and, in the boy's eyes, something has died. The same cold brutality is reflected in the faces of 15,000 children in Liberia. Children who are handed AK-47s and recruited to the killing fields of the eight year long civil war. Children as young as six.[13]

I recently talked to a staff member at World Vision in Uganda who had a hard time hiding his frustration as he told me of the failure of a programme to rescue child soldiers. The programme workers' efforts had seemed largely futile as each time they succeeded in a rescue, the soldiers would raid another village. Children who had just been rehabilitated with either their own family or a foster family, found themselves back with the rebels following another attack. Children were being recycled like paper. In Uganda the Lord's Resistance Army has been known to recruit children as young as five years old.[14]

Part of the boys' induction into life as a rebel soldier often involves being forced by their captors to harm or kill family members or peers. As for the girls, the higher an officer's rank, the more wives he is given. Not surprisingly, these young 'wives' are subject to sexually transmitted diseases.

Capture by a rebel army is not the only danger that children caught up in war can face. Between 1985 and 1995, 2 million children were killed, 5 million were disabled or brain damaged and 12 million lost

---

[13] *Tear Times,* Autumn 1999, p. 21.

[14] 'Girls Under Guns: The special situation of girl children affected by armed conflict — a case study of girls abducted by Joseph Kony's Lord's Resistance Army (LRA) in Northern Uganda,' a report for World Vision International, December 1995.

their homes as a result of war in their countries. In 35 lands, children were conscripted into the armed forces.[15] Another contributing factor to the active participation of children in war is the presence of small weapons. Many small weapons can easily be operated by children and these tools of war are responsible for up to 90 per cent of casualties in modern warfare.[16]

Such statistics reflect a drastic change in the nature of warfare over the last 100 years. At the turn of the century 90 per cent of the casualties of war were male soldiers. Today 90 per cent of the casualties of war are civilians, the majority of them women and children. One reason for this is that warfare in modern times is less likely to be conducted by one state against another, but is commonly a result of internal strife. Ordinary citizens, children among them, are subject to the terrors of war as manoeuvres take place in their own streets, their own villages, and they themselves are the victims. In Sierra Leone, for example, the losing faction in democratic elections has caused untold terror to ordinary civilians by engaging in brutal raids in which even small children have been targeted.

As war disables a country, deprivation and disease increase, and education ceases. In Somalia three generations have lost the opportunity to receive primary education, leaving the rebuilding of the country after war in the hands of an illiterate population unable to keep pace with the demands the twenty-first century will no doubt bring.

Cleansing a country from war takes time. The issue of anti-personnel landmines received great media attention, as the world became aware that children going out to the fields to play were dying or losing limbs because they either stepped on a mine or picked up mines resembling toys. The fields of many nations, such as Afghanistan, Mozambique and Angola, are not yet clear of landmines.

As a result of war, families are separated and torn from their homes. Save the Children estimates that 65 per cent of the 600,000 refugees from Kosovo were children.[17] Although many of the Kosovars were

---

15 *State of the World's Children* (UNICEF 1995).

16 *Tear Times*, Autumn 1999, p. 22.

17 Save the Children website, April 1999.

relocated within weeks, it can be years before refugees are able to leave the camps and shelters set up for them in neighbouring lands. Living in close quarters with thousands of other traumatized and displaced people, it is hard for parents or carers to educate children, gather enough food or protect against the diseases that can run rampant among such worn out and hungry people.

Children who grow up in war-torn lands are often traumatized and subject to untold psychological damage that continues to affect them as adults and consequently any children they may have. How can peace reign when war is all these children have ever known?

- 300,000 children are fighting in armed conflicts in at least 31 countries.[18]

- In some countries it is cheaper to buy a gun than it is to buy a book.[19]

- 1,000 children were killed between April and October 1992 in the war in Bosnia-Herzegovina and 1 million others lost relatives and homes.[20]

The slaves

Maria slips and hurts her foot again. But she picks herself up and carries on scraping through the mound of rubbish in Manila, the city once home to the infamous Smoky Mountain. The mountain has been bulldozed, but rubbish tips remain, populated by hundreds of workers who spend hours a day scraping and scavenging. Maria is one of them, struggling to earn the small amount that will keep her mother and younger sisters fed. It is worth her mother's while to send Maria out to work since six hours spent by a child on the rubbish tips is more lucrative than ten hours spent by an adult in a factory.

All over the world today children may be forced to work long hours not just by greedy and tyrannical employers, but by the families who depend on them for their survival. In some instances, children may

---

[18] *World's Children* magazine, Spring 1999.

[19] *Ibid.*

[20] *The Independent*, 11 June 1993.

be working to pay off a debt their families owe to a loan shark. The child's labour pays for the interest on the loan only, never touching the loan itself. These families are trapped in a cycle of debt, and their children are relied upon to keep pushing it around. And the children do keep pushing, because so many benefit from keeping them in work. UNICEF estimates that there are between 100 and 200 million child workers worldwide and says:

> Employers exploit child workers and use their ready availability to force down adult wages. Governments benefit from increased exports and economic growth. Families need the additional income provided by working children. Consumers at home and abroad enjoy lower prices of products produced with child labour. A shirt which can sell for $35 in the US can cost less than six pence in labour. By social conditioning and physical circumstances, children are more easily intimidated, more tractable and vulnerable than adult workers, making them easier to exploit and thus a source of greater profit.[21]

The African child is most likely to be involved in some form of labour, but the higher population of Asia means that there are more children working there. Nonetheless, child labour is a worldwide issue. Even in the United Kingdom, where mass child labour is now associated with Dickensian novels and where education is mandatory for the first 16 years, reports still arise of children working illegally, peeling prawns, packing jeans or wiring table lamps. Children in developing countries are typically drawn into a wide range of jobs in the fields of agriculture, domestic service, vending and manufacturing.

Girls have fewer opportunities than boys and often end up in domestic service, where they may find themselves subject to abuse. In India, for example, 58 per cent of girls work for nothing and 86 per cent of any income goes to their families, compared with 52 per cent of a boy's income,[22] although boys too may find themselves working for no pay. This is despite the International Labour Organization's Convention 138 on the Minimum Age for Employment (1973), which

---

21   UNICEF Information Sheet 'All Work and No Play: The scourge of child labour'.

22   UNICEF Information Sheet 'All Work and No Play: The scourge of child labour'.

states: 'The minimum age ... should not be less than the age of compulsory schooling, and, in any case, shall not be less than 15 years.' Developing countries are permitted to reduce this age to twelve where children are employed in light work only, but the nature of light work is undefined.

Children are cheaper to hire than adults, and in many countries it is culturally acceptable for children to be employed in some way. Few would complain about a child earning pocket money from an after school or weekend job, or even about a child working alongside his or her parents, learning their skill. Work in itself, where it is well monitored, can serve a healthy purpose, and where it does not interfere with a child's education it can be laudable. But when children are forced to work to survive, are exploited, placed under insufferable conditions, and denied education and healthcare either by people or circumstances, then the world must protest.

However, any attempts to take such children away from their jobs, no matter how appalling the conditions under which they work, could leave them worse off than before and less than grateful to Western well-wishers. When boycotts succeeded in closing down the garment factory in Pakistan where ten-year-old orphan Moyna worked to support herself and her grandmother, Moyna had to take to the streets to find an alternative source of income.

'They loathe us, don't they?' she said of the boycotters. 'We are poor and not well educated so they simply despise us. That is why they shut factories down.' She had no idea of the charity behind the boycotters' motives, just as the boycotters had no idea that the range of alternatives for children like Moyna is dire and that often the burden of supporting their families falls on their shoulders. For if you ask a poor man what his greatest resource is, he will answer, 'My children.' If you ask him further how best to help him, he will answer, 'Help my children. Unless their lives change, nothing in my life will change.'

Child labour is not only an inevitable consequence of the poverty faced by millions around the world, it is also a cause of poverty as children work at the expense of education. Because poverty rather than an understanding of the need for education drives them, closing down the factories that employ them will only cause them to search for work elsewhere, such as on the streets. As illness — especially the world-wide AIDS epidemic — brings death to impoverished families, more and more children are forced by circumstance into working for their family's living. How can these children ever hope to escape the cycle of poverty?

- An estimated 7 million children work in Brazil.[23]

- As many as 300 million children under the age of 15 are being exploited for their labour worldwide.[24]

- 70 per cent of child leather workers in Egypt work more than eight hours a day and only half of these attend or plan to attend school.[25]

The imprisoned

Marco is one-and-a-half years old and has never seen a flower. He lives in a prison in Lima, Peru, where his mother is an inmate, arrested for prostitution. He was born in the prison and may stay there until he is three years old. Once he leaves, he will rarely see his mother. When she is free she can claim him from the children's home where he will live when she can prove that she has a steady job and income, but with her background and prison sentence her chances of having her son returned to her are slim. Meanwhile, Marco's days are spent in fear as he fends off with childish aggression the dangers to his young person from the violent environment in which he lives. His sight is poor due to a lack of distant and colourful objects to look at, and, surrounded by women, he has no men in his life at all — no one to show him how boys grow up. But in one respect Marco is lucky. He does not have AIDS, unlike about a third of his fellow baby inmates.

๛ ๛ ๛

Children often follow convicted parents or guardians to prisons the world over where no alternatives exist for them. The horror stories of children who grow up without seeing blue sky, or hearing birdsong, or recognizing the image of a tree strike me deeply. In Uruguay, the

---

23   United Nations Children's Fund, Information Sheet, 29 March 1994.

24   ChildHope, Fact Sheet on Working Children.

25   United Nations Children's Fund, Information Sheet, 29 March 1994.

government acknowledges that children are placed in 'unsuitable' conditions such as prisons, hospitals or ill-equipped institutions. In Russia, orphans are housed in government institutions with extremely limited care. In North Korea, orphans face a similar situation and one can only guess the number of abandoned children housed by the Chinese authorities in appalling conditions. Channel 4's documentary, *The Dying Rooms,* showed a horrified world vivid pictures of Chinese children strapped to their seats and left unattended for days.

Meanwhile in Manila, five-year-old Francisco has been put into a youth reception centre. Francisco's home was on the streets, where he begged for a living, but the police took him in and now he finds himself in a 20 by 20 foot cell illuminated by only a small window, and filled with a number of other children, many of whom are older than him. The older boys take precedence over the younger in the jammed space and crowd close to the window, so that Francisco lives mainly in darkness. He cannot see clearly the faces of the 14- and 15-year-old boys who come up close to him, maybe several at a time, and he cannot talk of what they do to him.

A friend of mine, a university professor, once visited the prison in which little Francisco lives. As they met he implored her to get him out of there, to take him anywhere away from the darkness of his cell. In tears my friend recounted how all she could do was walk away as virtually no alternatives existed for little Francisco. The streets are harsh, but better than prison. In prison you cannot run away and you do not know how long you will stay there. Francisco is waiting for someone who cares enough to take his file and follow the paper trail of bureaucracy to ensure that he is released into a children's home. What will it take to help a child like little Francisco?

- In Rwanda, over 1,000 former child soldiers are in prison waiting to be charged for crimes they were forced to commit.[26]

- 50 per cent of those found guilty of criminal offences in the United Kingdom are under 21.[27]

[26] 'Children in Situations of Armed Conflict', Position Paper prepared by Dr Rainer Werning for the European Forum for Child Welfare 1998.

[27] BBC News, 26 September 1994.

- Between 1990 and 1994, 15 homeless children were killed in India while in police custody.[28]

The abused

Swe Swe is 13 and lives in a village deep inside Burma. Her family is very poor and often struggles to survive. One day Swe Swe is helping her mother when her aunt comes to visit, bringing with her a man Swe Swe has never seen before. They sit and talk with Swe Swe's mother for a long time while Swe Swe continues her chores outside. She cannot hear what they are saying, but sometimes she thinks she can hear her mother crying. Eventually, her mother calls her inside and tells her that she must go with this man. He will take her to a big city in Thailand to work as a waitress so that she can repay him for some money he has lent to her family. Swe Swe is glad that her family will not be hungry any more, but she is frightened and unhappy at the thought of travelling a long distance to an unknown place with this stranger.

Swe Swe is right to be frightened. The journey to Bangkok is long and undertaken by foot. At night she is housed in dark, unpleasant rooms and she receives only a little food along the way. When she gets to Bangkok she finds that her home is to be a brothel and her work not that of a waitress but a prostitute. Her family does not know this and should she manage to escape and find them again, they would most likely be too ashamed to have her back. A couple of times Swe Swe does try to escape, but on both occasions the police find her and return her to the brothel. She has no immigration papers and the policemen who catch her are her customers. They know where she lives. In the end she gives up trying to run away, discouraged by her burgeoning sense of shame and her inability to find her way back to her village, which she had never left before. She is in a foreign country and all around her people are speaking a language she does not understand. Neither can she read the road signs in the streets, which might tell her the way home.

---

[28]   Associated Press, New Delhi, India, 20 November 1996.

Swe Swe is just one of an estimated 10 million children caught up in prostitution, sex tourism and pornography.[29] It is further estimated that at least a million children enter this horrific trade each year.[30]

The same reasons that bring children to the streets can lead them into the sex industry, where they end up as tools for pimps or fodder for pornographers, all of whom are driven by greed for sex and money. Thailand is often cited as the worst offender, despite the fact that in November 1992 the Thai Government issued a policy on child prostitution in an attempt to halt the industry. It takes more than laws to change a problem of this nature as too many people have a vested interest in keeping the industry afloat. End Child Prostitution in Asian Tourism (ECPAT) estimates an annual turnover of US $1 billion in the child sex industry in the city of Bangkok alone, making prostitution one of the major sources of income for the city.

However, although Bangkok is notorious as a focus for paedophiles, child prostitution is a worldwide problem. From Bangkok to Birmingham, children are being sold for sex. In the United States there are around 150,000 child prostitutes.[31] In the coastal cities of Brazil, an estimated 500,000 girls under 16 are offered as part of sex holiday packages. The Children's Society revealed in a study in 1993 that girls as young as ten years old were selling themselves for sex in Britain's cities. Police in Birmingham confirmed that the prostitutes they were dealing with were younger than ever. On 29 August 1994, the British newspaper, *The Guardian*, stated: 'The price of children on the streets of Britain is falling, the sure sign that the supply has increased. A lot of older prostitutes feel threatened.'

The result of such abuse is as appalling as the fact. The Centre for the Protection of Children's Rights in Thailand estimates that 80 per cent of girls under 17 who have been rescued from brothels are HIV-positive.[32] The future that these children face is desolate. Removed from their families they are kept prisoners by pimps who do not hesitate to

---

[29] 'Children at Risk' No. 4, development education publication, World Vision.

[30] Eric Ram and David Westwood, *Together,* Oct–Dec 1996.

[31] ChildHope, Fact Sheets on Street Girls, March 1990.

[32] P. Green, *Prostitution: the victims* (unpublished 1994).

punish them if they fail to perform. They do not profit from their 'work' and they did not choose it, but it soon becomes the only way of life they know. They can do very little to change it, even if they have enough hope left to believe in alternatives. They often receive no education and the shame they feel may keep them from coming forward to accept any help that may be offered. The lives they live are loveless. There is no one to show them warmth and only rarely do they have good role models to prepare them for life. Any children they might give birth to are as much, if not more, at risk than they.

These girls are poorly housed and poorly fed, beaten, raped and prey to illness with little or no healthcare provided for them. Their very lives are in danger as some service as many as 30 adults a night, sometimes strapped to a bed. The first sexual encounter can kill a very young girl. Regular pregnancies and subsequent abortions are commonplace.

There seems to be two major reasons for this great demand for children in the sex industry. First, people who fear contracting sexually transmitted diseases, especially HIV/AIDS, only wish to purchase the services of virgins. This leads to ever younger children being drawn into the trade. To attract unwitting customers, cheap, ad hoc surgery and other measures are used to make girls who are not virgins appear to be so. Furthermore, a frightening rumour is circulating within this appalling industry that sex with a virgin is a cure for AIDS. Men who carry the virus seek out virgins, hoping to be cured by intercourse with them. The dark reality is that they only spread the virus further.

Second, I believe that the rise of web-based child pornography has contributed significantly to this problem. According to *Time* Magazine (April 1999) adult websites turn over more than US $1 billion a year and are becoming a massive growth industry. With this increased access to child pornographic materials, many who would perhaps never have ventured into this crime have been drawn in. What is worse, for many, watching and listening is not enough — it has to be tried. One of the most popular pornographic videos circulated in recent years was a video graphically demonstrating the gang raping of a group of children.

Any description of child sex abuse would not be complete without reference to domestic abuse. It happens across the world and is one of our last great taboos — a fact which makes it difficult, if not impossible, to grasp the extent of the problem. However, a study by David Finkelhor in the United States revealed just how widespread domestic abuse may be. From a survey of 800 students, Finkelhor discovered that more than 19 per cent of the females had been abused.[33] A similar study in Australia put the figure at 28 per cent,[34] while in the Netherlands another survey found that 33 per cent of females questioned had suffered abuse.[35] When a US Department of Health and Human Services study found a 100 per cent increase in the number of child abuse cases between 1986 and 1993, the Department Secretary, Donna E. Shalala, said: 'Now states, schools, health care officials — all of us — must commit ourselves to investigating and preventing child abuse with far greater effectiveness than we have seen in the past.' The study revealed that while girls are three times more likely to be sexually abused than boys, boys are at greater risk of emotional neglect and serious injury.

The Sri Lankan organization LEADS has conducted research which found that the staggering figure of 30–60 per cent of all girls in that country had suffered some form of sexual abuse in the ' safety' of their own homes. More research is being carried out and LEADS' dynamic director, Tony Senewiratne, says: 'These children cry in the dark and nobody hears or knows. Many will grow up to be future abusers in vengeance on a society which destroyed their innocence and youth.'

Although our emphasis has been on sexual abuse, domestic abuse may involve either physical or emotional abuse, or both. The perpetrators of domestic sexual abuse are often trusted individuals such as family members, close friends or people in positions of authority.

Sexually abused children often suffer from a great sense of guilt and remorse. They commonly fall into depression and believe themselves to be strange and different from others. Poor performance at school, self-mutilation or even attempted suicide can result and serious emo-

---

[33] D. Finkelhor, *Sexually Victimised Children* (New York: Free Press 1979).

[34] R. and J. Goldman, 'The Prevalence and Nature of Child Sexual Abuse in Australia', *Australian Journal of Sex, Marriage and the Family,* vol. 9, 1988, p. 94.

[35] N. Draijer, 'Seksuele Traumatisering in de Jeugd: Lange Termin Gevolgen van seksueel misbruik van meisjes door verwanten', Uitgerverij Sua, Amsterdam 1990.

tional problems throughout later life are inevitable. Take two-and-a-half-year-old Hayleigh's mother, Naomi. Hayleigh lived with her mum and dad in Plymouth, but Hayleigh's father beat her mother. Naomi was sexually abused when she was just a child herself. Robbed of a suitable male role model she is drawn to abusive men and can barely look after herself, let alone Hayleigh. The child is often found wandering the streets. Eventually, with the help of social services and a local Christian agency, Naomi finds a flat of her own in another town, but how long will it be before she is emotionally stable enough to protect Hayleigh and prevent further disruptions to both their lives?

As Donna Shalala indicated, prevention is the key to curing the world of abuse. For that to happen it is crucial that childcare workers and others in relevant positions are able to identify the symptoms and signs of abuse.

What will enable children like these to recover from the nightmare of their existence?

- 750 pornographic computer disks were seized by police in Dunstable from a school where they were traded by children as young as eleven.[36]

- In Sri Lanka, nearly all child sex victims are boys aged between 6 and 14.[37]

- More than 250 million copies of child pornography videos are circulating worldwide.[38]

The sick

Pedro's mother was a prostitute who abandoned him at the door of a hospital in Quito, Ecuador. Pedro has been in the hospital for 15 months. He was born without an oesophagus and must be fed through a tube five times a day. The nurses who care for him are busy and only manage to feed him three times a day. He is severely underweight and subject to frequent infections. When he reaches a normal weight

---

[36] *The Independent,* 23 September 1993.

[37] *The Independent,* 18 January 1994.

[38] *The Independent,* 19 January 1994.

and has gone three months without an infection, he can have an operation, but in the meantime, who will care for him well enough to ensure that this is achieved?

Pedro's short life is at risk even before it has begun. It is estimated that 33,000 under-five-year-olds die from preventable disease every day.[39] That is 25 children every second we live. UNICEF estimates that 2 million children die each year because they have not been immunized.[40] In 1990, the World Health Organization established the Integrated Management of Childhood Illness (IMCI) following the World Summit for Children. The Summit set the ambitious goal of reducing child mortality by 50 per cent before the year 2000 and recommended that five major child killers be the focus of attack: respiratory infections (such as pneumonia), diarrhoea, measles, malaria and malnutrition (see below). Seven out of ten child deaths are a result of one or more of these 'big five'.[41]

But there is another killer, one which has reared its ugly head in the last century. By 1994 alone, approximately 1.5 million children had been infected with the HIV virus.[42] The next generation is learning that sex is strongly associated with death. The AIDS virus has made sex a potential killer, while pregnancy often results in death either through abortion or risk to the impoverished and malnourished mother. Babies born to HIV-positive mothers may be abandoned as the shame and fear that accompany the disease cause the breakdown of family relationships. One-third of the children born to HIV-positive mothers are infected with the virus, and of those, 80 per cent die before they are five years old.[43] As more women become infected with the virus, so do more children. What is more, children born to sufferers of AIDS will in time become orphans. In Brazil, for example, it is estimated that 27,000 mothers will die of AIDS by 2002, leaving their

---

39   'The State of the World's Children', (UNICEF 1998).

40   'State of the World's Vaccines and Immunization' (Geneva: WHO/UNICEF 1996).

41   IMCI Information Sheets, Division of Child Health and Development (WHO, September 1997).

42   Sue Armstrong and John Williamson, 'Action for Children Affected by AIDS: Programme Profiles and Lessons Learnt' (WHO/UNICEF Joint Document 1994).

43   Alison Rader, 'Children and HIV/AIDS', in Phyllis Kilbourn (ed.), *Children in Crisis* (MARC 1996).

children at risk and displaced. Eight per cent of those children will be infected themselves.[44] With such a poor start in life, those who do survive have little chance of a comfortable life. Orphaned children have no one to advocate for them, no one to provide healthcare or ensure they get an education. They are unlikely to inherit land or money to establish them in life. They are alone.

Malnutrition is an even bigger killer. It accounts for 55 per cent of all child deaths each year, which means that 17 million children are dying every year because they are hungry and therefore susceptible to death from usually non-fatal diseases.[45] Malnutrition is more than just suffering from hunger. If the body fails to receive vital micronutrients a child will either die or develop severe problems. These micronutrients may only be needed in the tiniest amounts, but a lack of iodine, for example, could damage a child's intellect. Lack of iodine in the mother could produce a still birth and even endanger the mother's life. The mother is also in danger if she lacks folate, while her child could suffer from a birth defect such as spina bifida. Vitamins are essential to the growing child. Without Vitamin D the bones will not form properly — a problem particularly prevalent in countries with long winters such as Mongolia — and a lack of Vitamin A could result in blindness, as well as leaving the child susceptible to diarrhoea and measles, both conquerable but often killers in the developing world.

Micronutrients are needed to produce the enzymes and hormones required by the body to regulate biological processes such as growth, and the development of the immune and reproductive systems. For example, a lack of zinc could lead to delayed sexual development in boys.

These are just a few examples of how a lack of micronutrients hinders a child's development and reduces his or her quality of life. There is no cure for children already suffering from these problems. Since they did not receive the necessary forms of nutrition in the womb or in early life, it is already too late to protect them and those who survive have to live with the consequences.

---

[44] Miguel B. Fontes, Janette Hilis and Glenn K. Wasek, 'Children Affected by AIDS in Brazil' in *Children in Crisis.*

[45] United Nations.

Like child labour, malnutrition is not only a result of poverty, but also a cause, as the malnourished children who grow to be adults may nevertheless die young, leaving their own children orphaned. Malnourished children find it harder to interact normally with other people and have a harder time forming fruitful relationships. A malnourished mother is unable to breast feed her child and if she is HIV-positive this necessarily deters her from feeding in this way. But if she also lives in a region where the water supply is polluted, she cannot rely on breast milk substitutes, which are mixed with water, to feed her child.

We have seen how malnutrition can cause disability in a child, but whatever the cause, disability can subject the disabled child to neglect and abuse by both family members and society at large. Adults are often embarrassed by malformed children. Families hide them away believing the disability to be a form of curse. Disabled children often have less access to facilities and education and are thus less able to participate as fully as possible in the social and economic life of their community. Very few initiatives address the special needs of disabled children, even though some of them suffer from ailments that may be eased or even cured. For example, the former mayor of Bulawayo, Zimbabwe, Joshua Malina, spent the first twelve years of his life crawling around the floor of his mother's hut, uneducated and isolated, before he was reached by a missionary.[46] According to Rachel Hurst of Disabled Peoples International, only 2 per cent of children with disabilities in developing countries receive any form of rehabilitation.

Child health is a massive issue and continues to be a challenge for the future. What can we do to better preserve the gift of life?

• The United Nations Children's Fund calculated that money spent by western Europeans on cigarettes every six months (that is, £14.5 billion sterling) would effectively control all childhood diseases, halve the rate of child malnutrition, bring clean water to all communities and provide most of the children of the world with a basic education.

---

46 Rachel Hurst, Disabled Peoples International. Submission to the Committee on the rights of the child: thematic day on disabled children, 6 October 1997, p. 3.

- Every day 400 to 500 Zambians are infected with the AIDS virus.[47]

- The infant mortality rate per thousand is 7 in northern Europe, 51 in South America and 108 in eastern Africa.[48]

A great problem or a great God?

As we consider these stories and statistics, it becomes clear that though the sufferings of children the world over may be varied, the root causes interweave to tell one dull tale of misery. Poverty leads to family breakdown, which often leads to abandonment, which takes children onto the streets or into other volatile situations such as exploitation, slavery or prostitution. Poverty, exposure and abuse will often cause poor health, very early parenthood or death.

An old friend and I once found ourselves with a Filipino street educator under a bridge in Bogota, Colombia, some time after midnight holding a brand new baby. Standing there amid a group of street children, in the din of downtown traffic, with a 13- year-old mother and a 14-year-old father put a whole new perspective on childcare issues for us. Themselves born on the streets, the parents of this child were less than prepared for what was to come. My Filipino colleague was desperate to find shelter for this little child and soon found it in an ill-managed government children's home. However poorly run or unsuitable, it was at least safe, reasonably clean and provided regular meals.

The stories and statistics of children in need both overwhelm and challenge us. They ought to! The stories of Pedro, Maria, Swe Swe and the other children described here can be repeated a million times over with different names and from different places. Each one of them fills me with grief and pain. Yet as I consider these children I cannot but admire their struggle for life. They are more than simply worthy causes for our compassion. They are people with a very real chance to make a lasting difference in their own lives and in the lives of the people and communities around them. We must give them that chance.

---

[47] 'World Pulse', Action International Ministries, 3 October 1995.

[48] United Nations Population Fund.

For most people 'children in need' is nothing more than a marginal issue — just one topic of concern among the many facing the world today. However, I believe it is essential that the Christian movement gets involved in reaching these children as a reflection of the importance our Lord puts on them, and as a sign of the integrity of our message. For surely, if the gospel is our salvation it must be demonstrated by the way in which we live and care for our families, our communities and our children.

As the eighteenth-century philosopher, Edmund Burke, said, 'It is necessary only for the good man to do nothing for evil to triumph.' And the prophet Isaiah indicated what we can do:

> The Spirit of the Sovereign Lord is on me, because the Lord has anointed me to preach good news to the poor. He has sent me to bind up the broken-hearted, to proclaim freedom for the captives and release from darkness for the prisoners, to proclaim the year of the Lord's favour and the day of vengeance of our God, to comfort all who mourn, and provide for those who grieve in Zion — to bestow on them a crown of beauty instead of ashes, the oil of gladness instead of mourning, and a garment of praise instead of a spirit of despair. They will be called oaks of righteousness, a planting of the Lord for the display of his splendour. (Isaiah 61:1–3)

God's Response   3

You are the light of the world. A city on a hill cannot be
hidden. (Matthew 5:14)

As we look at the needs of the world today we cannot ignore the fact
that there are more children than ever before and this means that more
children than ever before are at risk.

The fact that children are in need all over the world is motivation
enough for us to act on their behalf. Wherever Christians and children in need exist in the same place, there is action. Any humane person would be moved by the plight of these young people and many,
both Christians and non-Christians, have given up everything to make
life better for the children who have been brought to their attention.
Yet Christians have special reasons for getting involved and extend-
ing the love of Christ to children.

A biblical mandate

Christians are a people with a mandate, a commission. One thing I
have pondered at great length in my Christian walk is what it means
to have a mandate. For me it boils down to a biblical command. From
cover to cover of the Bible God warns us not to harm his children because they matter to him.

In Lamentations 2:19, Jeremiah makes a heartfelt call to those who
will listen. 'Arise, cry out in the night,' he says, 'as the watches of the
night begin; pour out your heart like water in the presence of the Lord.
Lift up your hands to him for the lives of your children, who faint from
hunger at the head of every street.' This is a clear, biblical mandate
from God to all who call him Lord to be involved with children in need.
I will look at ways of doing that later in this book, but here at least we
can consider Jeremiah's call to prayer. Not just a call to prayer either,
but to a heartfelt cry of compassion which we know the Lord will hear.
We know he will take notice of what we ask because the Bible is full of
commands to share God's love for children. This is part of what loving

and obeying him means and I believe that God longs for us to appreciate the extent of his concern.

Consider: 'See that you do not look down on one of these little ones. For I tell you that their angels in heaven always see the face of my Father in heaven' (Matthew 18:10). Scripture warns against seeing children as insignificant. God's perspective is the opposite of the worldly mindset which tends to regard children as less important than adults and therefore low on the priority list. When the disciples tried to keep children away from Jesus (they probably thought he did not have time to be bothered with them), Jesus was indignant. He did not want the children kept in the background. Not only did he rebuke the disciples and specifically call the children to him, but he pointed out that children have something to teach adults: 'Anyone who will not receive the kingdom of God like a little child will never enter it' (Mark 10:15). In their simple faith and responsiveness, children exemplify kingdom principles.

Similarly, Jesus used children as examples when teaching on greatness: 'Whoever humbles himself like this child is the greatest in the kingdom of heaven' (Matthew 18:4). He continually challenged the prevailing opinion, which views those with wealth and status as important. To Jesus it is the 'little ones' who are the greatest.

Jesus loved children because he knew that God is a father. As one who called God 'Abba', meaning father, his goal was to bring all people under God's fatherly care. The careful nurturing of children and the principles of family lie at the heart of his relationship with humankind. It is by calling believers not just his people but his children that God shows how important we are to him: 'How great is the love the Father has lavished on us, that we should be called children of God!' (1 John 3:1a).

Children are precious, and as such are to be protected and cherished. Terrible consequences await anyone who harms them: 'But if anyone causes one of these little ones who believe in me to sin, it would be better for him to have a large millstone hung around his neck and to be drowned in the depths of the sea' (Matthew 18:6). The protection of the fatherless is mentioned again and again in the Old Testament too. (See, for example, Deuteronomy 10:18; 14:28–29; 24:17; Psalms

82:3; 146:9; Proverbs 23:10; Isaiah 1:17.) God is quite clear: the penalty for the exploitation of widows and orphans is death. He says: 'Do not take advantage of a widow or an orphan. If you do and they cry out to me, I will certainly hear their cry. My anger will be aroused, and I will kill you' (Exodus 22:22–24a).

Again in the Old Testament, Israel's practice of child sacrifice arouses God's fury: 'You slaughtered my children and sacrificed them to the idols. In all your detestable practices and your prostitution you did not remember the days of your youth, when you were naked and bare, kicking about in your blood' (Ezekiel 16:21–22). How does God feel, then, when children's lives are sacrificed daily as a result of our idols of self, money and ambition? Remember the dreadful stories related in the previous chapter and consider them in the light of these Bible verses. If we are too appalled even to take these stories in, let us mark that God the Father is also appalled and let us share in his response. As the 'Oxford Statement on Children at Risk' says: 'Our own anger is but a pale reflection of God's own fury and indignation. Our compassion for hurting children and the righteous anger that arises within us reflects nothing less than the jealous love and righteous anger of our heavenly father.'

However, God is not just appalled, he is active. He likens his treatment of Israel in Ezekiel 16 to the rescue of an abandoned baby, who had been despised and thrown out into the open field: 'Then I passed by and saw you kicking about in your blood, and as you lay there in your blood I said to you, "Live!" I made you grow like a plant of the field. You grew up and developed and became the most beautiful of jewels' (vv.6–7a).

Each of us has a story to tell about how God has intervened in our own lives, some more dramatic than others maybe, but all of us know that God has done something for us and hope and trust that we have begun to be like a beautiful jewel in his eyes. When we follow Christ, his deeds become our deeds. As he has rescued us, so we have a moral responsibility to be involved in his rescue of others. 'This is love for God: to obey his commands. And his commands are not burdensome' (1 John 5:3). If God is the Father of the fatherless and if we are followers of him, his ambassadors and representatives, then children who are at risk should become our children.

My wife, Emily, and I were married for five years before we had children and as we travelled around the world people often asked us
whether we were parents, especially when we visited countries where
having several children is commonplace. We usually answered that
yes, we had about 100 million children, but they all lived on the streets.
People generally paused and then laughed when we gave this answer,
but we did not mean to be flippant. We do consider those children to
be our children, our responsibility.

We find this idea that God is the Father of the fatherless expressed
particularly strongly in Psalm 68, a song of King David about a great
and wonderful God. So often we see God as the God of the poor, as if
that is something else that he does. But here David flips that idea on
its head and says that the first wonderful thing about God is that he is
a Father to orphans. Being Father of the fatherless is one of God's highest attributes. It is a core part of God's character to look after children
and he adopts us as his own sons and daughters. We are not just ad-
herents of a code or a faith; we are his children, the family of Christ –
and so are the children out there who need us.

What is more, children in need are not to be seen as a mass problem,
their identities merged into one faceless blur of difficulty. Our own
experience of God has taught us that each person has intrinsic worth
because they have been created in God's image. Not only that, but
they are unique. Nobody is replaceable, and nobody, least of all a child,
should be treated as disposable. Psalm 139 reveals the precision and
tenderness with which God forms every individual: 'You created my
inmost being; you knit me together in my mother's womb' (v.13). Born
or unborn, young or old, each person is a work of God, 'fearfully and
wonderfully made' (v.14) and is to be cherished.

Just as God is a Father with a family, so he has ordained the fundamental unit of society to be the family, to reflect heavenly relational
principles. God intends children to be nurtured within a loving family. The family unit, based on a man and a woman living in faithfulness to one another in the divine institution of marriage, is the environment in which children can grow properly and receive the care
and training they need. Parents are responsible for teaching their children carefully, bringing them up 'in the training and instruction of
the Lord' (Ephesians 6:4) and for giving appropriate discipline. Like-

wise children are called to honour their parents.

The church, as a wider family, has a responsibility to provide support, protection and nurture to children, especially where the natural family fails or abdicates. The church is to serve as God's agent. What is asked of us is active involvement, not simply passive concern. Psalm 82:3–4 is typical of the Bible's cry for action: 'Defend the cause of the weak and fatherless; maintain the rights of the poor and oppressed. Rescue the weak and needy; deliver them from the hand of the wicked.'

The New Testament confirms that action is what God requires: 'Religion that God our Father accepts as pure and faultless is this: to look after orphans and widows in their distress' (James 1:27). A Christian faith is worth nothing without practical concern for others. Jesus' command is: 'in everything, do to others what you would have them do to you' (Matthew 7:12). If you were trapped in a life of poverty and exploitation, would you prefer to be ignored or to be offered a way out?

Christians are called to be salt and light: salt, to act as a preservative in society, preventing moral decay; light, to help people to see the truth of who God is – to see his incredible love, mercy and compassion. Both of these commands confirm our responsibility to children in need. Stopping decay in society involves stopping evil from being meted out to children, and enabling people to see who God is involves putting his love and compassion for children into action. When we take on God's nature, others come to know him through us. We believe in a gospel that is practical – this gospel of good news for the poor, freedom for prisoners, release for the oppressed.

Ephesians 2:8–10 explains that while we are not saved by good works, we are saved for good works, having been 'created in Christ Jesus to do good works, which God prepared in advance for us to do'. If we love God we want to be like him and to do the things he does, becoming his co-workers. Jesus' work is all about deliverance and rescue, in practical as well as spiritual terms. Psalm 72:12–14 looks forward to the reign of the coming king, 'for he will deliver the needy who cry out, the afflicted who have no-one to help. He will take pity on the weak and the needy and save the needy from death. He will rescue them from oppression and violence, for precious is their blood in his sight.'

Love and kindness are among the hallmarks of true Christianity. Christians are called to reflect these qualities. 'Live a life of love, just as Christ loved us and gave himself up for us' (Ephesians 5:2). Paul reiterates this in Romans 5:1–5 when he points out that 'God has poured out his love into our hearts by the Holy Spirit, whom he has given us' and nails it down in Romans 8, triumphantly stating that 'we are more than conquerors through him who loved us' (v.37). It is this love which prompts us to care for children at risk.

A Legacy of Transformation   4

A new command I give you: Love one another. As I have
loved you, so you must love one another. (John 13:34)

The good news is that from the days of the earliest church, followers of Christ have been actively involved in caring for children in need. Efforts in Christian childcare today are not just the result of the rise of the parachurch movements that responded to the Korean crisis in the 1950s – a move that has brought such modes of intervention as child sponsorship to the fore. No, such efforts have been a hallmark of genuine Christianity for 2,000 years.

As we have seen, Jesus placed a strong emphasis on children, and members of the early church were instructed to involve their children in worship and to bring them up according to Christ's teachings. In 1 Corinthians 7:14, Paul describes as 'holy' those children born even to parents where one is a believer and the other is not. In Acts 21:5, as Paul and his companions leave Tyre for Jerusalem, it is the whole body of believers, men, women and children, who send him off by praying with him on the beach before departure.

For early Christians, then, parenting involved teaching children about Jesus and this provides a model for modern parents and for all who seek to parent children. As Jesus taught and healed children, so the early church followed his example, leaving us with a tradition that has passed through the ages giving us many examples of how (and sadly, in some cases, how not) to care for children today. For example, first-century Romans might have left unwanted babies (such as those born the wrong gender or with disabilities) on dung heaps or rubbish tips to die or be picked up by those who might exploit them, but Jews and Christians were known for putting a different value on their children's lives. No Jewish or Christian child would have been exposed in this way. Neither would they have been in danger of death at the hands of those who brought them to birth, nor of being aborted before being given the chance to live. In fact, some Christians would do more than look after their own children. 'The Christians were strongly opposed to child exposure, actively rescuing foundlings, and deplored abortions which they did not think defensible except with arguments that equally justified infanticide.'[1]

Care for the poor was a common feature of church life for Roman Christians, and the poor inevitably included widows and orphans, for whom hospices and homes were set up. In the middle of the third century one Roman church is recorded as caring for 1,500 widows, and a church in Syrian Antioch in the late fourth century is remembered for feeding 3,000 hungry people. No distinction was made between Christians and non-Christians when it came to serving the poor. It was the need of the individual that motivated church members. This tradition continued throughout the ages, taken up in the West in the Middle Ages by monasteries and convents. Monasteries were also a source of education and provided an alternative life to children of the nobility who otherwise would have entered the military.[2]

By the time of the Enlightenment, the role of Christianity in promoting goodness was in many ways taken for granted, so that writer, Jonathan Swift, could say: 'We need religion as we need our dinner, wickedness makes Christianity indispensable and there's an end of it.' Known for its introduction of rationalism into modern thinking, the Enlightenment was not so destructive to the church as is commonly imagined. It was the clergy who caught up the new spirit of the times and encouraged the people to read and write in order that they might benefit from devotional literature. Women began to be acknowledged as a powerful influence in church life, particularly in the running of schools and hospitals. With their elevation, children began to be seen as individuals rather than just small people. The church was responsible for a spread of charitable institutions and voluntary societies across western Europe, precursors to the great wealth of Christian organizations that sprang up in the Victorian age. It is said that the slave reformer, William Wilberforce (1759–1833), was a subscriber to around 100 such organizations – a testament to the strength of a social movement that included projects for orphans, lying-in homes for poor women, homes for climb-

---

[1]   Henry Chadwick, 'Early Christian Community', in John McManners (ed.), *The Illustrated History of Christianity* (Oxford University Press 1990).

[2]   Adrian H. Bredero, *Christendom and Christianity in the Middle Ages* (Eerdmans 1994).

ing boys and Irish serving girls and criminal poor children. Meanwhile the church was actively engaging in mission and spreading such good works abroad as far afield as Africa and China (albeit to what is now acknowledged to be mixed effect).

Some of the most famous Victorian philanthropists must be mentioned by name. Lord Shaftesbury, for example, devoted his life to charitable work among a range of society's poor, including child workers such as flower girls and chimney sweep boys. His 'ragged schools' for poor children have gone down in history.

Elizabeth Fry, the Quaker famous for her prison work, first became aware of the great need in England's prisons when she was asked to make baby clothes for the children of inmates in London's notorious Newgate, so vividly depicted by Charles Dickens in several of his novels. Appalled by what she found, Elizabeth Fry set up a school inside the prison and began to hold services. Her work prompted a reformation of the entire English prison service.

Edward Rudolf, founder of what is today known as The Children's Society, began his mission when, as a Sunday school superintendent in Lambeth, London, he noticed the thousands of street children who roamed there. Likewise, Dr Thomas Barnardo, a medical missionary in the same city, was made aware of the conditions in which children lived when a destitute boy took him to all the places where his companions slept out, even in winter. Dr Barnardo, whose charitable organization also continues his work today, is particularly remembered for his promise never to turn a child away from one of his homes. By the time he died in 1905, he had helped nearly 60,000 children.

After such strong testimonies to the power of Christ when his people begin to do his work, we almost need not mention William Booth and the Salvation Army, George Muller and the orphanages he began in his adopted home of Bristol, and Robert Raikes, a key proponent of the Sunday school movement, which taught working children to read and write alongside lessons from the Bible. In the USA Christian social action found an expression in organizations such as the Gospel Tabernacle, a New York church established by A. B. Simpson, whose programme of outreach included orphanages at home and in India, and which eventually generated a whole movement of churches dedicated to social action, known as the Christian and Missionary Alliance.

Again in New York, the name of Emma Whittemore will for ever be remembered as the founder of the Door of Hope Union, a rescue project for what were then known as 'fallen women'. Emma Whittemore opened her first home in 1890 and by the time she died in 1931 there were nearly 100 homes providing shelter, food and love to women of the streets. Evangelism was a prime objective of Mrs Whittemore, who was known for saying that although the girls might get out of vice, 'only Jesus can get the vice out of the girls'. She also encouraged converts to become evangelists themselves.

It is not only Western countries which can claim success in the cause of childcare, however. Korea, mentioned above as a focus for Western Christian attention when war broke out in the early 1950s, had established its own Christian movements long before then. The Bible Club, for example, was founded in 1930 for children of poor families who could not afford to attend school. These establishments offered an education centred around the Bible and they continued to serve their purpose when the war 20 years later left many children orphaned or destitute. Through the Bible Club thousands of children were given an alternative to the way of life so common to children in need. Many children who attended the Club became evangelists themselves as they went home and shared what they had learned with their families. Seoul, the capital of South Korea, is today famous for having the largest Christian congregation in the world.

In India a remarkable but little known childcare pioneer, Pandita Ramabai Mukthi, a Brahmin convert, was responsible for the Mukthi Mission near Pune, Maharashtra, founded in the 1870s.

So we see that throughout the ages up to the present time Christians have taken up the mantle of Christ and become living testimonies to his care and compassion for the weak of this world. This is a mantle that continues to be worn by Christians today.

The church's work today

Part of my work over the past seven years has involved extensive travel all over the world. During this time it has been a great honour to witness the extent of Christian work with children in need in virtually every culture and context. We saw in Chapter 2 that the problem of children in need is vast, yet the church is a vast resource, which, if fully mobilized, is capable of addressing the needs effectively. In fact, the church is the largest movement working on behalf of children in need today in terms of children reached, ministries established and workers on the ground. In one Indian state alone (Tamil Nadu) there are already 1,500 childcare projects run by Christians.

Most of this work is little known. The scale of the church's work in the field of children in need is often a surprise to people, even to those within the church. Quietly, numerous individuals around the world have become involved, investing time and money often at great personal cost, and have gained valuable expertise. Collectively, a huge body of experience and skill has been accumulated. Projects have grown and developed, ideas and methodologies have been tested, and valuable lessons have been learned. The challenge today evolves around harnessing and accessing this potent resource.

With experienced workers and well-trained professionals already in the field, a good foundation for future development is in place. What is more, these workers are motivated by a desire to be Christ's representatives. They are not just Christians who happen to be involved in childcare. They are childcare workers who are ministering the gospel of Christ to children.

They are people like Eyiba Yamaria, Co-ordinator of a budding children in need ministry linked to Viva Network in the Democratic Republic of Congo. He has set up a Sunday school in his church which not only teaches children about Jesus but also feeds them, clothes them and enables them to attend school.

Or people like Ingrid Wilts, Founder of Child Restoration Outreach in Uganda. Ingrid works in a day care centre for street children which provides youngsters with a place to go during the day, offers them counselling and, where possible, helps them to become reconciled with their families.

In Malawi, Gastin Gachepe, another children in need ministry network co-ordinator, gathers street children together and teaches them the gospel. In Nigeria, Pastor Musa of the Believers' Anointed Covenant Chapel visits children in hospital. Some of these children are unable to pay their hospital bills and Pastor Musa's church helps them out with practical difficulties such as these, as well as bringing them the message of Christ.

Jean Webster works with orphans for a project called Church Community Orphan Care connected to the Evangelical Fellowship of Zimbabwe. Her role is twofold in that she works with the orphans in the home and also mobilizes local congregations to seek out needy children in their own communities. Volunteers then make visits to the children, pray with them, offer them resources, help them with healthcare issues or just with practical jobs around the home. Her work, she says, is 'about caring for these orphans in the communities where they live and helping the churches to realize that they can resource the needs they find'.

Jean has heart-warming tales to tell about some of the children who come under her direct care. Despite suffering from desperate illnesses, the children, she says, have moved her to greater faith in God. Take infant twins, Joshua and Joanna, for example, both of whom escaped abortion before birth, and one of whom, Joanna, is HIV-positive.

'They were supposed to be aborted,' Jean says. 'The grandmother gave her teenage daughter medicine, but in the end the twins were born two months premature. They were put in a box, no clothing, no food, just put in a box with the placenta to die. It was June, it was cold. After 48 hours the village health worker found them. They had frostbite on their hands and feet.'

Eventually the twins were brought to Jean. Throughout her young life, Joanna has nearly died several times, but the prayers of staff and children at the orphanage have sustained her. 'Little Joanna has a heart of care,' Jean says. 'She's stubborn, she's going to be a leader, she's also going to be a nurse. If anybody falls she's the first one to say sorry and strengthen them. Little Joshua has got such a voice and remembers songs. He sings "What a faithful God have I".'

Apart from Joshua and Joanna, Jean also makes special mention of a small boy who came to the orphanage at the age of three with cancer of the eye. 'When he was five or six, it came back,' Jean remembers. 'We prayed. He never complained. You'd ask him how he was and he'd say, "Fine." Only on the last day would he say, "I'm tired," or "I'm sick." He went in his sleep. In the midst of all his pain, I broke my arm. I went to see him with my arm in plaster. His growth was almost bigger than his head, but he reached out and prayed for my arm in all his pain. These children are beautiful. They just love Jesus.'

In the United Kingdom, centres such as the Canaan Christian Centre in Norfolk, established by Evelyn Smith in the late 1970s, offer a refuge to children from troubled homes. Some of the staff at the centre come from countries around the world as volunteers offering their services to children like Shane and Marie.

When their father was taken to court everyone hoped he would be given a prison sentence. Instead he got probation. Understanding the life-threatening nature of the situation, the police and social services assisted Shane and Marie and their mother, Sandra, in making their way to the Canaan centre, hundreds of miles away from their own home. Here the family could stay while they learned to rediscover the joys of safety within an environment that offered opportunity for safe play, for an ordered life of going to school and helping out with little jobs like feeding the rabbits and for counselling, until eventually Sandra, Shane and Marie were able to move into a home of their own.

The Living Springs Family Home in the Midlands works in a similar way to the Canaan Christian Centre so that when baby Josie came to stay at the home with her mother, Susan, she was able to recover from the trauma she had already endured in her short life. No one knew how, but Josie had been subjected to a beating. Her whole family was invited to stay at Living Springs where Josie would be observed closely. Susan stayed with Josie, while Josie's father, David, lived at home but spent all his time at Living Springs. In this safe and warm environment the family were able to spend time together under observation for Josie's protection and to become members of the wider household that constituted Living Springs.

As Josie recovered and bloomed from the love and attention she was receiving, David was able to confess that he was responsible for her injuries and to receive counselling for the frustration that had overcome him as he tried to care for a crying baby. Eventually the family were able to return to their own home together and Josie was able to grow up in a home where she could know she was loved.

Shane, Marie, Josie and the other children mentioned here received the kind of love and support it is only to be hoped they would receive from children in need ministries. The staff at the Canaan Christian Centre and Living Springs work tirelessly to care for the children who come to them. But there is another kind of children in need ministry worker; a kind who may not see a child all day.

Josefina Gutierrez works for the Philippino Children's Ministry. A typical day for Josefina, as she described it to us, began with telephone calls to contacts in the local Christian childcare community. Josefina spent an hour following up ideas in this way before participating in an extended meeting with her counterparts from other agencies to brainstorm on how to mobilize support for the Worldwide Day of Prayer. (This happens annually on behalf of 'children at risk' on the first Saturday in June.) After the meeting, Josefina made several visits to network contacts, dropping off letters, providing briefs and learning more about the work done by local ministries as well as sharing with them ideas which had arisen within the existing network. As the day drew to a close, Josefina continued to pursue contacts by writing letters from home to possible supporters of her work.

Unlike Pastor Musa or Jean Webster, Josefina does not spend her days working directly with children, and this is true of a number of other colleagues in the Christian childcare community. 'The body is a unit, though it is made up of many parts; and though all its parts are many, they form one body' (1 Corinthians 12:12). Without people working behind the scenes and facilitating contact between childcare workers, children could not be helped so powerfully.

Josefina believes that she has been called to her work by God and that what she did on the day in question 'will help mobilize prayer support for children at risk'. She says:

> The more prayers are generated for the children and for the various work that is done among them, the more we can expect God to move in mighty ways and the more we can expect to see greater things accomplished. Christians should know and be convinced that the work done among children is not simply a response to children's need to survive but an act of obedience to God's command to bring them to him, because the kingdom of God belongs to them. This should

help the church put children at the top of its mission agenda.

Second, there should be a willingness to work together if we are to see breakthroughs in this huge task.

Josefina's work is echoed in the Viva Network International Co-ordination Office by Sonia Wilson, Networking Manager. Sonia's days are not unlike Josefina's in that her tasks also largely involve linking up with colleagues in the Christian childcare community to motivate, encourage and learn. On one typical day, Sonia linked up a funding group with a children's project in Colombia, began planning for a forthcoming co-ordinators' training session, linked up a potential supporter with a project in Malawi, talked and prayed over the telephone with Viva Network's co-ordinator in Slovakia and worked on the co-ordinators' monthly news service. Sonia did not see a child all day, but her work was vital in improving the quality of care given to children the world over.

'People who are encouraged and envisioned to continue working will be better workers for the kids,' Sonia says. 'And when networkers are trained effectively they can provide better support for project workers. The link up with funders is obviously important – when projects are well funded they have more opportunity to help kids.'

Sonia's involvement stems from her own experiences of grass-roots childcare. She has known children in great need of physical, emotional and spiritual help, and, like myself, she has witnessed projects on the ground struggling to survive for lack of training, funding and the sharing of resources.

This awareness of the needs surrounding children at risk and those who seek to care for them is a key motivation for all Viva Network's contacts in the Christian childcare community. Raymond Samuel of the Society for Integrated Social Upliftment (SISU) says that he came to childcare because of his own experience of being cared for as a small child. Later he found further reason to give his life to God in thanksgiving. 'I dedicated my life to serving the Lord after he saved me from a tragic accident,' he says. 'My goal is to save children from neglect, poverty and abuse and to provide them with an opportunity to experience Christ's love.'

Raymond is involved in childcare for what Katharine Miles calls 'the long haul'. Katharine started her ministry in the childcare community in Mexico, working among street children in the city of Puebla, and later joined the embryonic efforts of Viva Network's International Co-ordination Office in Oxford. Now she operates from Miami, as Latin America Co-ordinator for Viva Network. Her work is not dissimilar to Josefina's or Sonia's and its purpose, she says, is to mobilize, encourage, prepare and resource workers who are keen to devote a large portion of their lives to ministering to children. 'I want to see a movement of prayer mobilized throughout Latin America so that the body of Christ can fulfil her mandate to reach children in need with the gospel of Jesus Christ in a united and effective manner,' Katharine says. 'The church is doing so much to help children, but there is so much more that we could easily do.'

The church's potential

Katharine is right to say that the church is active in the field of childcare. Current Christian involvement in childcare projects is massive. Unfortunately it represents only a tiny proportion of the worldwide church. According to Dr Peter Brierley, Director of the Christian Research Association, there are at least 2.3 million local congregations across the world. A vast number of these are as yet unmobilized in the area of children in need. The potential for growth in terms of church involvement is huge and as the rate of church growth itself is high, especially in the Two Thirds world, the opportunity for new ministries to emerge is increasing.

These local congregations include church members who are part of virtually every strata in society, often trained and experienced in a variety of relevant skills, such as healthcare, construction, law, finance, administration, management and so on. There is also a tradition of working together on projects and a fair amount of property strategically positioned in towns and cities.

The Christian movement, through the presence of local congregations, could comprise one of the greatest opportunities for effective childcare in the next century. I will discuss this at greater length later.

Global, co-ordinated involvement in childcare has never been easier.

Travel and communication are constantly improving, making it possible for people on opposite sides of the world to work together effectively. Air travel is coming down in price, computers are becoming increasingly affordable and portable, and email provides a cheap and rapid channel of communication. Information sharing, awareness raising, and consultation between childcare projects are now much more possible. Information on organizations working on behalf of children in need can be accessed by simply browsing their websites on the Internet, for example. Such advances in travel and communication are a source of great opportunity for the church in its efforts to reach these children.

The only question that remains is: What is standing in our way of doing more?

> And if anyone gives even a cup of cold water to one of these little ones because he is my disciple, I tell you the truth, he will certainly not lose his reward. (Matthew 10:42)

Gaps in the Wall 5

You see the trouble we are in: Jerusalem lies in ruins, and its
gates have been burned with fire. Come, let us rebuild the
wall of Jerusalem, and we will no longer be in disgrace.
(Nehemiah 2:17)

Ian de Villiers gazed out of the window of the crowded train as it rumbled through the Indian countryside. He sighed, remembering his conversations at the different children's ministries he had just been visiting. More than half of them had never even heard of other projects very near to them, even though they were also run by Christians trying to meet the needs of children at risk. As he reflected, he prayed for the workers he had met. The vast majority of them were almost as traumatized as the children they served. Not only were they suffering from sheer exhaustion, they also felt isolated and unsupported. They were overwhelmed by the constant demands from the children at their feet, by the need for fundraising and staff recruitment, and by the ever growing task of developing an efficient administrative system to deal with their varied tasks.

The problems that Ian encountered are not unique to Indian Christian childcare projects. Despite the great capacity of the church worldwide to meet the needs of children at risk, there are still vast numbers of projects that fail and workers who are unsupported. Projects tend to be driven by a small number of highly committed individuals, often involved at great personal cost. They face the enormous challenge of running an effective childcare project while lacking sufficient resources and the mental and spiritual space to deal holistically with the children they seek to love. These children come to them traumatized and unhappy. Listening to their stories requires strength of mind and spirit; a strength which too often is sapped by the daily demands of their work.

Any questions they might have, such as 'Who does what where?', 'Who can help me with a, b or c?', 'Who has done this before?', 'Where can I find out about...?', 'How do I do. . .?' are constantly ignored or at best given incomplete answers for lack of time, resources and contacts. But issues of childcare, management and resource acquisition are essential to functional childcare. Questions regarding how to care for staff, how to care for the children, how to deal with growth and how to form relationships with donors, law-makers, the law enforcement authorities and others in the community are an integral part of helping children.

Establishing a professional childcare project among children in need is not dissimilar to establishing a small business. The death and closure of most projects can be traced back to mistakes made in the first couple of years of their existence. Exact figures are unknown, but my own research and consultation around the world has led me to believe that the majority of new projects, perhaps as much as 75 per cent of indigenous ministry, collapse within the first 24 months. The stress and strain of pioneering work with children at risk more often than not gets the better of the pioneers' goodwill as, overworked and disillusioned, they acknowledge that the conditions for their project were just not right. To begin work with children in need is a tall order, but to do so in isolation, with no useful contacts or experience, is nothing short of a miracle. The nagging question staring any Christian childcare worker in the face today is: 'How do we make it easier to respond to the needs of children?'

In the Old Testament book of Nehemiah, we read of the gates and wall around Jerusalem being broken down and ruined, leaving large gaps open to marauders. In the same way we recognize failures in the Christian response to children in need. It is time to rebuild the walls and ensure that Christians not only do the job but do it well.

In order to be the best at what we do, we must be honest about our shortcomings and about the difficulties facing segments of the community. Problems that have not first been identified as such cannot be solved. Let us therefore take a brief look at some of the issues facing the Christian community of outreach to children at risk, keeping in mind that any description of a global community will necessarily be drawn with broad brush strokes. It is my hope, nonetheless, that the images portrayed will prove illuminating to childcare communities locally.

Prayer

The greatest need facing every member of the Christian childcare community is the need for prayer. I have been astonished at the number of childcare workers who have cited this need as their most urgent. It seems that virtually everyone agrees: prayer precedes power! And power is precisely what is required to tackle the problems faced by children at risk: godly power to be as the Lord desires us to be in order for us to do the things he calls us to do.

The Greek word for power (*dunamis*) and the Greek word for authority (*exousia*), as used in the Bible, have two fairly distinct meanings. The latter means 'to have permission', the former 'to have the ability'. The difference can best be explained by a short story: An official visiting a farmer brought with him a document granting him permission to enter the farmer's field. The farmer wryly informed the official that he was welcome to inspect the field, but that he should beware the bull that lived there. The official had the permission, but did he have the courage to enter the bull's territory? It is evident that the church has a biblical mandate, permission from God if you like, to respond to the needs of children at risk, but it often lacks the ability. Perhaps the best prayers we can pray would be for this kind of power.

Prayer is also the gateway for involvement. When we pray for something we are far more likely to get involved. The exciting thing is that all Christians everywhere can pray and achieve great results by doing so. Rebuilding the walls of Christian childcare will involve informed, concerted and compassionate prayer at all levels of the Christian community.

In Paraguay, one of the first tasks of the new network was to set up a telephone prayer chain. Whenever a child disappeared, or resources were lacking, or a project worker fell ill, for example, one person called the next in the chain, who called the next and so on. With a minimum amount of effort and organization, a very simple initiative proved highly effective.

In Cape Town one day, the telephone on Karen Hinder's desk rang. Karen, a Welsh missionary working for the local city childcare network, had developed a similar chain to the one in Paraguay and, once again, the initiative was to prove useful. On the other end of the telephone was a distraught project director who told Karen that the project's minibus had been stolen overnight. The theft severely hampered the project's ability to perform its function. It was essential that the minibus be found and returned. Karen called her group of intercessors and a number of other projects in the network to ask for their prayers. The next day she visited the project to be met by the director with tears of thanks. Not only had the minibus been found, but in the meantime many other project workers across the city had called to offer encouragement and the loan of their own minibuses.

The value of this kind of support may be hard to quantify, but in this instance prayer not only worked in that the minibus was returned, but it also strengthened the network members' sense of belonging to a supportive group.

Prayer can also unite Christians in different parts of the world as together they are effective in their care and concern for those at risk. In Chapter 2 I talked of Pedro, who was born without an oesophagus and was poorly cared for by nurses. I asked who would care for him. The good news is that Pedro did attract the support of a couple who adopted him and brought his plight to the attention of their community, both in Ecuador and in their homeland of Holland. No one could deny the severity of Pedro's condition, but as his adoptive father says, 'If God doesn't do anything else through Pedro's life, he has caused hundreds of children to pray. There were probably a couple of thousand children all over Holland praying for him. It has taught me also.'

Another remarkable story of the power of prayer is that of Beatrice, who was found lying on a dirt road in Mozambique by Heidi Baker of Iris Ministries. To any casual passer-by Beatrice was not an attractive sight. Heidi describes her as having 'a bloated belly, red eyes and worms coming out of her toes'. She was also suffering from a skin disease. But as Heidi stopped to pick her up she was touched to the core. 'As I looked into her eyes, I saw Jesus in her. I hugged her, but she didn't really want to be touched.' Later Heidi discovered that Beatrice had been raped in the past. She was going blind and her chances of survival were slim, but 'many prayed for this treasure'. High doses of Vitamin A restored her sight and eventually Beatrice recovered and was able to attend school.

'Beatrice became one of the most compassionate children I've ever met,' Heidi says. 'She wants to give her life to missions and working with street children in Mozambique.' She goes on to recount how Beatrice was instrumental in the recovery of another young girl, Constancia, who as a result of abuse and abandonment was silent and never spoke. Beatrice adopted Constancia as a companion and gradually the two children began to know something of what child-hood can be. 'My favourite picture is of Constancia and Beatrice play-ing with hula hoops, laughing and singing,' Heidi recalls. 'When it comes to mind I think, "Wow! They can be children again."'

Isolation

Isolation is perhaps one of the biggest and most crucial problems to face Christian childcare projects. When my colleagues and I began researching existing ministries for children at risk in Guatemala City, for example, we discovered that there were 42 projects. The excite-ment of that discovery was somewhat tempered by the further rev-elation that only four of them had the required *personeria juridica:* their legal licence to work as a non-profit organization. That meant that 38 Christian childcare projects could legally be accused of kid-napping children.

The bottleneck in this particular incident was a result of the cost and time involved in getting the required permit. The projects knew they needed to operate legally, but simply could not find the $2,000–3,000 needed to get their permit. As this need was identified, efforts were launched to find a lawyer. Once found, this Christian man volunteered his services free of charge and more projects began to gain legal sta-tus. Problems similar to this could be solved if projects everywhere were linking together, comparing notes, sharing information and re-sources, and helping to lift the weight off each other's backs.

A problem shared by many Christian ministries is that they lack knowl-edge about what is available and happening in the world just outside their own door. For example, in one town, councillors had to decide what to do with two purpose-built orphanages in need of staff and leadership. They offered the responsibility for running these orphan-ages to a local pastoral fraternity. The churches were pleased to be asked and accepted, even though they had had no experience in handling this type of work. Their efforts failed and they were asked to hand the homes back to the city council. At the same time, and unbeknown to the pastors, one of the best run orphanages in the entire region was located in their city. Had they known, the required expertise and some human resource could have been drawn from the link. To everybody's chagrin and disappointment they realized that they had missed an ideal solution because of the lack of communication and co-operation between local Christian bodies.

Raymond Samuel, the director of an indigenous Indian childcare project, recounted to me another such tale of woe. He had been working in Maharashtra, distributing nutrition supplements to save malnourished tribal children from dying in some 40 villages in remote hills which for two years had been affected by drought and later by severe rains. Children were starving and more supplies were needed urgently. Raymond contacted several distribution agencies but found no response. Six months later the situation was even more serious, but eventually the largest church relief agency in Bombay, which he had approached a year before, offered supplies. Having watched 450 children die in a matter of weeks, Raymond was desperate and felt elated when he discovered that all the supplies he needed were just ten minutes from one of his branch offices in the same state. Elation turned to dismay, however, when Raymond and the agency representative found out that the supplies were now three months past their expiry date. Had Raymond known of their existence during the height of the famine those 450 children might have lived. Instead the food, the product of hard work on behalf of the fund-raiser, had gone rotten.

When Viva Network helped to facilitate the launch of a network in Argentina, we held a conference for all the Argentinean Christian childcare ministries we could find at the time. As is usual at such conferences, everyone present stood up to introduce themselves. One man described himself, with a note of pride in his voice, as a representative of 'the only prison children ministry in Cordoba and probably all of Argentina'. Then he sat down. The man next to him took his turn with a somewhat bemused smile on his face and proceeded to describe himself as 'the second only prison children ministry in Cordoba and probably all of Argentina'.

While stories such as this amuse, they also highlight the frightening sense of isolation among Christian groups doing similar or identical work. People who do not know about each other do not speak to each other and therefore never learn from each other or simply encourage each other over a cup of coffee every now and then. In one of St Paul's letters to the Christians at Corinth, he encourages them to share their resources with the suffering church in Jerusalem. He writes:

> Our desire is not that others might be relieved while you are hard pressed, but that there might be equality. At the present time your plenty will supply what they need, so that in turn their plenty will supply what you need. Then there will be equality, as it is written, 'He who gathered much did not have too much, and he who gathered little did not have too little.' (2 Corinthians 8:13–15)

St Paul's words are a challenge to all of us to share the riches we have and to give, both materially and spiritually, to those who have less. But it is also an instruction with practical consequences. When we share, everyone benefits in the long run. So often, even among Christian ministries in close proximity to each other, the unequal distribution of resources leads to waste. A large donation of day-old bread, for example, will not last for ever. If several feeding projects in the same area can share their surpluses, then more children can benefit and the time will come when the group who received the first time may be able to give. Likewise, the failure of Christians to show a unified front to the wider community has many consequences. Many public bodies are simply unaware of the potential of Christians in their locality and never think of consulting them on vital matters concerning children, or allocating public funds for their work.

In some cases local authorities, sadly, have been put off because of feuds or bad feeling between different denominations or groups, each trying to hold its own at the expense of the other. This not only affects the provision of resources for children, but also our witness to the love of Christ in the whole community. When Christians do connect and unite on issues of policy, they can become a formative body and have a far greater impact in the shaping of laws affecting children. What is more, as the story of the orphanage reveals, the church at large is often ignorant of the needs of these ministries, even of ministries on their own doorstep. When they do act, it is important that their response is appropriate, with ongoing training and consultancy.

The cost of this ignorance is high. Ultimately it means failure to meet the needs of children at risk and to share the goodness of Christ in the world. Who has all the knowledge needed to run a soup kitchen, care for street children, rehabilitate war-damaged children, or minister to children in prison? These are skills that are learned over the course of hard experience. When Christians are not linked together, every new situation that arises, no matter how common, must be dealt with as though for the first time. Devising teaching plans, approaching local authorities for resources, finding prayer support, tracking down sources of food, funding and equipment, dealing with legal problems, enforcing discipline, figuring out how to handle emotional upsets with staff and children... with each new problem the wheel is reinvented in an attempt to find solutions. Without the experience and accumulated wisdom of others to draw on, mistakes are made that could have been avoided.

Wesley Stafford, President of Compassion International, once told me how he had visited three different street children ministries in three different cities of Brazil. He was there to evaluate which of these three projects would win the support of Compassion.

The first project impressed him with the thoroughness of its plans and the model of intervention it sought to follow. The second project made an equally strong impression. Wes asked the project workers there if they had heard of the first project or knew anything about its method of working. While not having heard of the project themselves, they not only knew about the method it employed, they had spent the past four years trying to get that model to work and had failed miserably. They started pointing out the various problems and errors of this model and left Wes somewhat shaken by the fact that highly committed people in a city not far from where he sat were about to commit serious time and resources to get a defunct model off the ground. He left for his third stop and had a frightful sense of *déjà vu* as this final project ventured to explain its ideas and plans. When asked if they knew of the other two projects, they confessed they did not, but when introduced to the two models reviewed previously the third group explained that they had tried both and failed. Shaken to the core, Wes suddenly realized the enormous benefit a meeting could have for the three groups in question. How much grief and waste could be avoided if they had the opportunity to meet, even just once!

Precious time and energy are uselessly poured out trying to discover solutions to very common problems, while a limited amount of money drains away on unnecessary expenses. In the same way, sharing resources can avoid unnecessary duplication of work. For example, the time involved in finding a campsite suitable for a holiday for children can be used more effectively if the knowledge is shared among groups. Such shared knowledge made all the difference to one 15-year-old boy in Uganda. He had left a troubled home life to live on the streets, but regularly attended a project run by Child Restoration Outreach. Through the project he was put in touch with another group which organized camps. Six weeks on one of these working camps took him off the streets and when he returned he was a changed young man. He decided to return to his family home and ask for his family's forgiveness for disappearing for two years. His stepmother accepted him back into the family home and was soon commenting on the change in her stepson. Life continued to be difficult for him, but he was off the streets and making a difference in the lives of those around him.

I do not think it would be much of an overstatement to say that everyone involved in reaching children in need has too much to do and too little with which to do it. It must therefore be our first priority to maximize the use of our resources and minimize the extent to which we duplicate efforts or reinvent wheels that have long since proved unable to perform.

Pursuing excellence

My first encounter with children in need was as a 17-year-old worker on a project in Latin America. From this experience I know how valuable a relatively short-term involvement can be, both to the worker and to the project. However, nothing can replace permanent staff. There must be skilled permanent staff to run the project if the children are to receive the ongoing help they need. I kicked a ball around with the kids and helped to keep them generally amused, and, not least of all, it was while there that my heart was impressed by the tremendous needs of both children at risk and childcare workers. But beyond playing with the children there was not much that I could do. In many projects, a number of the workers may be very young and inexperienced. Full of enthusiasm, they nonetheless lack the knowledge and skills to deal effectively with the complex problems of children in need.

Lack of effective planning, sufficient resources and trained staff means that most childcare projects could be accused of operating unprofessionally. Most projects start in heartfelt response to immediate need and are often not carefully preconceived. They simply happen.

A North American missionary by the name of Greg Saracoff exemplifies this kind of response. With a Mexican friend he decided to go to the streets of downtown Tijuana in Mexico. His friend was a local pastor who ran a children's home with 27 beds. Once in the city centre they discovered a group of street children and started witnessing to them. At the end of the evening five of the children made a commitment to leave the streets. What could Greg do? The pastor believed he could squeeze an extra two children into his home, but three still needed housing. There was simply no way Greg could find it within himself to leave the children there, so he called his wife, Kathy, and asked if she could prepare some extra for dinner.

Soon Greg and Kathy discovered that these three children had brothers and sisters who also needed a home and some dinner and before they knew it they had started a ministry to the street children of Tijuana. In Matthew 5 Jesus calls us to be the salt and light of the world and that is exactly what Greg and Kathy were trying to be. Their ministry did not stem from years of planning. It just happened. However, when I met Greg a few months down the road, he was one very large question mark. 'How do I...?', 'Where can I find...?', 'Who has done this before?', 'What happens when... ?' were just a few of the questions buzzing in his head.

Once up and running the need to be professional becomes acute. Children at risk need more than just to be reached — they need to be raised by adults who treat them as their own children. One of the great challenges facing the Christian community of outreach to children in need is to find ways of combining the enthusiasm, the get-up-and-go of the Christian movement, with the experience and professionalism acquired through 2,000 years of caring for children. The children we serve need more than our enthusiasm; they need the longevity of effective holistic care.

During my time in Latin America I all too often witnessed the heart-rending scenes of children walking, hand in hand, back into the slums and the red light districts surrounding the park we worked in. Despite all our goodwill and good intentions we had no way of providing housing for the homeless, shelter for the fearful, food for the hungry or education for those trapped by poverty.

Worse yet, we were unable, at that time, in that place, to find answers or even begin to ask questions about how to care professionally. Like many of our peers today, we were thrust into a situation we did not understand, disconnected from those who did, and unable to begin the process of developing a meaningful response.

The Book of Zechariah exhorts us not to 'despise the day of small beginnings', yet while we recognize that all ministries must start somewhere, we must also have a commitment to move beyond those small beginnings and develop what it takes to help the children we are called to serve.

Ministry performance standards

One helpful tool to take into consideration is the identification of good practice. What does good Christian childcare look like? What it involves, how it is achieved and who is doing it are all helpful issues that can be summarized in a code of best practice. It is, however, important to keep in mind that each context and culture creates a unique environment and any code of conduct or practice should reflect this. The best ministry performance standards are often created through local need analysis and through participatory reflection of on-site grass-roots practitioners. Once standards have been established and agreed upon these ministries are ultimately the ones to keep each other mutually accountable, as together they pursue yet higher excellence in ministry. This type of examination of self and peers can, if carefully managed, be a very helpful, if sometimes humbling, exercise. The formation of networks is again essential for this to happen.

It is hard to build a peer group if you do not know where your peers are, or if you do not trust them enough to be vulnerable. Furthermore, to arrive at the stage of being able to develop and implement ministry performance standards requires a carefully facilitated process, which can normally only be carried out by someone dedicated to the task of networking or facilitating the network. It takes an informed, neutral 'go-between', as everyone else is naturally too consumed by commitments to their own ministry.

While needing anchorage locally a need remains to identify 'best practice' internationally. Broad guidelines for good ministry would be very helpful for local groups to look at as a starting point for their own discussions.

Training

Professionalism, or capacity-building as some would call it, must naturally involve training. Viva Network has in recent years pioneered an initiative to develop an international certificate of children at risk studies. This course is split into four modules and involves extensive time in model projects as well as in the classroom. Initially run by reputable training institutions in nine different countries, we hope that this course will multiply itself through the network of Christian training institutions worldwide.

The certificate course is primarily geared towards the full-time student, which leaves currently committed childcare workers out of the equation. They are often not able to spare even one day a week away from their project site and thus would be better served training in smaller chunks that are more specifically directed to the needs faced in that particular locality. Interactive workshops and other events, as well as distance learning courses, regular publications or manuals are typical examples of what is required for helping existing staff.

The other important element of this type of training is the need for a local network of groups and individuals involved in this field of ministry. Only when a sense of community is developed and a network of organizations begins to identify similar needs does training of any kind become practically possible. It is, after all, easier to organize training events for 50 people rather than five. I have been part of forming more than 25 local networks and one of the greatest needs always identified is the need for training. Time and again project leaders cry out, 'I don't know what issues I'm dealing with. I'm not prepared. I got pulled into this by my compassion.'

The vast majority of people I have met during eight years of research into the needs of Christian work with children at risk have been humble enough to realize their need for capacity-building. The great news is that most childcare workers eagerly await expertise and advice. The problem is in providing it.

As we enter the twenty-first century the Christian church stands at the top of the list of candidates willing and able to handle the global privatization of care, education and welfare. However, if the church is to continue expanding as the major service provider in these and related areas, we need to make sure that we do so with the highest possible level of integrity and professionalism. We do not want to be simply good enough — we want to be an exemplary model of how to care lovingly and effectively for children in need.

In order for this to be achieved, two things need to happen. A deep sense of the needs must grip everyone involved in this field of ministry, along with a recognition that training is part of God's call on our lives. Christian enthusiasm has much to commend it, but it can at times cost us more than we thought we saved by our activism.

Second, since few projects can spare the workers they have to a lengthy course, training must be made accessible locally and appropriately. It is no use, for example, giving graduate level training to people who are great with kids but can hardly read. Even less useful is training in a language unfamiliar to the target audience. Ultimately, the achievement of high standards in Christian care for children in need is possible. The Christian movement certainly has the experience, the know-how and the technology required. It is simply a question of getting the job done and recruiting more people to do it.

Caring for the caregivers

A very serious but often unrecognized problem for people in the front-line of ministry to children in need is lack of practical, emotional and spiritual support. Inability to find time for fellowship with other Christians, or for personal renewal, and lack of prayer backing lead to discouragement and early burn-out. Some carry on, but begin to lose the vision they once had for helping these children and end up investing all their resources in just surviving the next crisis. While we would seek to increase the number of Christian childcare ministries, before that can happen in any great way, let us ensure sufficient support for existing projects. How can we ask God for more if we do not look after what we already have? Christian ministries are not known for their care to caregivers. So often, those who join a mission agency or childcare organization ditch their careers by doing so. They travel to some far-off place where they have to make cultural adaptations (admittedly this may be part of the appeal), are overworked and underfunded and probably lack the ideal qualifications and experience for the type of work they are doing. The Christian movement is notorious for making emotional sales pitches to people who should never get involved in childcare.

Caring for caregivers begins with the selection process. A rigorous screening process would give both the applicant and the employer a chance to evaluate personal motives and sift out those who are interested for the wrong reasons. If a candidate does not have the right motivation or experience, he or she can care as much as possible but will be of little use once on site. This is proved by the high turnover of childcare workers. Ian de Villiers was sighing his prayers on his Indian train journey because he had seen evidence of this on his travels. While short-term workers, if properly treated and trained, can have real value, children are in need of parental figures who will stay the course. All children need a mum and a dad.

It is the breakdown of relationships that often puts children at risk. Restoring or instituting long-term relationships with children is our key task. Ultimately, children at risk need more than social workers; they need mums and dads who will love and respect them as they are, despite all their problems. Childcare workers are in many ways more than simply childcare workers. They are pseudo-parents who establish close relationships with the children under their care. As we are told in 1 John 3:1, we are 'children of God' because the Father has lavished love on us. What an example for our own dealings with fatherless children!

That is why the selection and training of childcare workers is paramount. Well-chosen, well-trained and well-supported childcare workers are more likely to stay where they are needed. All of our pence, pounds, policies and programmes are rather pointless without the childcare workers. They are the noblest part of what we do, which is why it is so shocking to see the level of neglect they endure as they struggle bravely to meet the overwhelming needs that face them each day.

Has God Gone Bust?   6

The kingdom of God does not come with your careful
observation, nor will people say, 'Here it is,' or 'There it is,'
because the kingdom of God is within you.
(Luke 17:20b–21)

Money is high on the list of needs. Too much to do and too little to do it with. Too many children to reach and not enough money with which to reach them. This is the reality for Christian childcare projects all over the world as the vast majority just scrape by from week to week, making do with almost, often not quite, enough.

Has God gone bust? Is it just that scrabbling around for resources is a fact of life? Maybe the Lord has exhausted his ministry expenses account, or perhaps he is trying to teach us something by the fact that we only just get by?

I believe the Christian movement has the potential of mass expansion in its efforts to reach children in need. I am a convinced optimist. I truly believe that we will see a radical change in Christian efforts to reach needy children worldwide and that millions of children will find help and comfort as a result.

However, I am also aware that something fundamental needs to change in the way we underpin these efforts financially. Currently most ministry to children in need does not reflect the sufficiency, indeed the victory, of our Lord. Rather it is affected by the compassion fatigue felt by Western donors weary with good causes clamouring at their doorsteps for attention and support. Even where there are generous givers, funds raised from donations alone never quite meet the need, let alone offer enough support to engender an explosion of ministry in this field. Radical change is required.

While most Christian childcare is done by local people, much is run by cross-cultural missionaries, who can often run into problems peculiar to their situation. Take, for example, Carey. Although she is fictitious, she is representative of many foreign missionary childcare workers I have come across in countries all over the world.

Carey feels the call of God on her life to move to a Central American country and begin working with street children. She gathers what support she can and makes the move, braving the rough world of street kids to the extent that she virtually lives with them. As time goes by she begins to form relationships, then to teach the children their letters and eventually she feels that the time is right to provide some sort of shelter for the new friends she has made. Up until this point Carey has needed little money to do her work. It does not cost much to live on the streets. But now she needs to increase her funding base to give the children what they need. Her first port of call, naturally enough, is her church back home. They have supported her thus far and are glad that her work is expanding. Yet Carey's new project is in Central America, not Boston, USA, and she would really like to get local churches involved in what she is doing. Her home church's support is precious but limited and she does not know how long she can depend upon it. It is going to take more than a garage sale or a coffee morning to raise the sort of capital her project needs. Carey finds herself spending increasing amounts of time away from the children on fundraising trips. She has to find extra staff to care for the children and so her fundraising needs increase. She has become a fundraiser rather than the street worker she set out to be. What is more, initial enthusiasm over her project is waning as potential supporters grow cynical and demand evidence of its credibility. Carey finds herself stretching the same old stories, trying not to mention the many times things did not work. In an effort not to be dishonest she falls back on vague generalizations. Her motivation is slipping and she cannot remember when she last worked a full night with the kids. What is more, despite all her efforts she never seems to be able to raise enough money.

Carey's story outlines some of the problems with distance funding. The tension between quality versus quantity is often decided by the donor, who wants value for money. Value is more often than not measured in numbers rather than in the quality of care offered by the various projects. That children sometimes 'graduate' from the programme only to return to the slum they came from, where they have illegitimate children who eventually end up at the same home their parents left only years back, often remains a story untold. Children may leave projects having received only a sub-standard education and without the extended family network that often proves crucial in helping them to get jobs, housing and a social life. A donor-driven view of childcare is not politically correct, but it is practical and often the only alternative to closure.

What is more, while projects rely solely on donations it is likely that, like Carey's project, their income base is miles away from the project itself. Although Carey is an example of an independent missionary, many foreign workers are supported by Western-based organizations. An enormous apparatus is needed to distribute and justify what funds are donated. Time and money must be spent on sending Western representatives out to projects to ensure that the public's donations are being well spent. Good reports can encourage further giving, but such check-ups are secondary to the task at hand: reaching children in need. Childcare workers and organizations are being asked not just to perform their difficult task of reaching children, but also to develop systems of accountability and fundraising, which is a whole different ball game. It is a very expensive way of doing what we are seeking to do. It is far better to fundraise locally where a higher level of trust and accountability can be established. It is also better if the people who spend the money collect it. In this way they become far more accountable to their donors, because these donors are local people who understand local needs.

God has sufficient power and ability, through human agents, to make things change. God can solve this problem. He can, of course he can. Believing this, we can put our creativity, talents and all of our resources into making it happen. If we do not, our ministries may finally crumble, not just from lack of money, but from the disillusion and weariness that come when we seem always to be fighting the same battle and always losing.

At present, Christian childcare benefits from private donations, government funding or income-generating projects and larger business ventures. Child sponsorship is a major source of funding and is fronted by large well-run missions, as well as the better-known agencies such as Compassion International, World Vision and TEAR Fund New

Zealand. In fact, it was World Vision which introduced the concept of sponsoring a child to the Western well-wisher. While on a preaching tour in China in the late 1940s, a young American evangelist, Bob Pierce, was invited by a Dutch schoolteacher, Tena Hoelkeboer, to preach to the children at her school. Bob accepted the invitation and spent four days with the children, at the end of which he encouraged those who had made commitments to Christ to go home and share the good news with their parents.

The next day, Bob went to take his leave of Tena only to be met at her door by an appalling sight. In Tena's arms was a bruised and beaten child. Her name was White Jade. She had followed Bob's advice and told her parents of her new-found faith. It had cost her her family and her home. In anger, Tena demanded to know what Bob planned to do to help this little girl. Bewildered, he could only offer the five dollar note he had in his pocket and agree to Tena's request that he send five dollars every month to help her raise White Jade.

Bob Pierce later went on to found World Vision, and sponsorship as a method of support was formalized by World Vision in Korea in 1953 as a response to the number of children orphaned during the Korean War. It continues to be a popular means of giving with Western donors who can now choose from a range of organizations offering it as a solution both to the problems of children in need and the donor's own need to reach out to the wider world.

Despite the success of child sponsorship and the wide range of other sources of income, there are problems, and two key new trends are causing us to revisit the whole area of funding. One is that phrase we are all tired of hearing, the aforementioned compassion fatigue. The other is increasing recognition by local government bodies of the place of non-governmental organizations in community care.

Private donations

Traditional charities have complained of a declining income, despite recent recoveries in the world financial markets. It seems that the public is overwhelmed by the knowledge of all that is wrong in the world. They gave and gave when they first heard of famine, but the troubles keep on coming: war, natural disaster, disease. What more can they do? In the less-developed world people often give far more sacrificially than in wealthier parts of the world. Compassion fatigue is largely a Western problem. Consider, for instance, the Englishman, Jim Brown.

Jim Brown is a worker who gets a reasonable salary and gives away a small percentage to a good cause. In order to maintain Jim's sympathy, the charity of his choice must spend time and money convincing him that their work is worthwhile. They know that every week Jim sees advertisements in newspapers for other charities or even gets their literature through the post. Any day now he could decide that he likes another charity better. Jim has only a limited amount to give away and he wants to choose carefully.

What the fight for Jim's support requires is a constant drive to produce a better poster, more emotive photographs and more heart-rending wording. What it results in is competition between charities, even between charities fighting for similar causes — a situation both unhealthy and often ungodly. Professional fundraisers talk about the roof, or the pool, of monies available for fundraising. It is only possible to squeeze the donor to a certain extent, and once the limit is reached it is simply tough luck.

One day, a sudden and unexpected natural disaster occurs in a part of the world Jim is particularly interested in. A disaster relief fund is set up and Jim sends his monthly cheque to the fund instead of to his regular cause. Thousands like him all over the country decide to do the same thing. Others, who never give on a regular basis, send a one-off donation to the newly destitute, never considering that what they can spare that day could be spread out over a longer period of time and given to a charity each month. Money is flowing in to the disaster area and other ongoing causes are left dry. The pool is exhausted and empty. But it need not be a pool. It could be a river. It needs to be a river!

More and more valid applications for funding from third generation Christians in developing countries for excellent projects, which really merit funding, are landing on desks of donor bodies. All of them are saying, 'We really want to care for these children.' But the donor community can only shake their heads in despair, knowing that they only just have enough money to meet the projects already on their lists.

Charitable funding, to my mind, will probably never be enough to meet the need unless there is a world revival. The USA is known to be the most charitable country in the world, and its evangelical population is its most giving part. The average amount given by this caring community is 2.38 per cent of their earnings, a figure far lower than the biblical suggestion of a tenth. In the southern hemisphere, the concept of charitable giving is even more difficult. Not only do people generally have less to give, the idea of giving to a charitable organization is a new concept, making fundraising exceedingly hard for indigenous charities, although this is beginning to change. It is impressive to see what has been done with so little means, but it is clear that donor support will never be enough to sustain and enhance the work.

Surely here lies a challenge for every preacher! If giving is an integral part of Christian life it should be encouraged vigorously. A friend of mine once burst out, 'If I was required to pay 10 per cent of my income under the law of the old covenant, what should I not be willing to pay under the grace of the new?' If every new Christian sponsored a child, if we all collected our small change and gave it away, if we actually paid a tithe and on a regular basis, we would start to realize that he who gives is more blessed than he who receives, and the world would change. Jesus demonstrated the powerful lesson of God's faithfulness in this area when he admonished his listeners: 'Give, and it will be given to you. A good measure, pressed down, shaken together and running over, will be poured into your lap. For with the measure you use, it will be measured to you' (Luke 6:38).

However, while private giving is wonderful, it is not our only option for raising funds. We can also examine how best to use our skills and time to generate a self-supporting income for our projects. I believe that if more organizations gave income generation grants rather than administrative grants, projects could be financed more adequately. Instead of an annual grant being awarded to a favoured orphanage in, say, Beirut, which provided for a certain amount of food or clothing, the orphanage would receive a lump sum. This it could invest in a bakery, a car park or other project, which would generate income on a long-term basis. Rather than simply provide an endowment with a fixed yield, this model releases another segment of people into service and ties the dynamics of a business venture to that of a charitable one. It provides income and sometimes training for the children and young people in the project and may eventually offer them a job, and it further provides the added value of being seen as a charitable business, selling bread or parking cars to help the children of our cities. Talk about market advantage!

This model could reduce and eventually eradicate the need for ongoing support to the project. It would also free up the sum presently allocated to public relations in a London or Berlin office, say, enabling the project to focus on its all-important work at home.

One hurdle to overcome in pursuing this model is the need to differentiate between the charity and the business. There should be a clear division of labour between each project's childcare workers, who are focused on and dedicated to delivering good childcare, and its business staff, who are focused on and dedicated to developing a healthy business. The last thing we want to do is load more onto the backs of already overworked childcare staff. Rather, the benefit of such a model is that it relieves them from the duty of fundraising since they can rest secure that the business wing of their project is doing that job for them.

It is important to observe that a lot of businesses fail, and even if they succeed, they do not always make sufficient profit to contribute substantially to a charitable enterprise. It is also important to identify the different functions of business and charity and not try to merge the two and thus achieve little. The business wing of a project will surely fail if it is run along charitable lines. It must be shrewd in its dealings, while existing to support the charitable wing of the project. But while this model of income generation is not without its drawbacks or difficulties, it has the potential to take projects much further, much faster than any other financial tool.

This is, of course, not a new idea, but very ancient. In previous periods the church has been dependent upon funds generated from business ventures, and can become so again. In modern times, Scripture Union's street children project in Lima, Peru, has led the way. From the outset they established a bakery, a car park and a city bus service. Each month, after paying salaries and overheads, the business makes a profit out of which the project is run. Last time I was there the manager, Paul Clark, asked me to terminate the funding links that I had established for the project with another organization in Denmark, since they no longer needed this support. This is quite unusual! I would be happy to hear a lot more requests like that.

Government funding

Second, governments and inter-governmental agencies are recognizing the importance and validity of non-governmental organizations (NGOs) as primary service providers in the areas of health and social welfare. Whether it is the Norwegian, Danish or Canadian governments who acknowledge the value of Christian work in their overseas development budgets, or the city councils of Cordoba, Nairobi or Miami, the message is the same: Let's outsource where possible!

The logic of this hangs together, as voluntary organizations often give governments and local councils more value for their money. These organizations are more likely to be free from corruption, and using them saves councils the cost of their own overheads. What is more, NGOs are largely self-motivated and employ staff whose commitment stems from their convictions rather than their desire for financial reward. Government agencies are realizing like never before that you cannot purchase compassion, but only encourage and support it where it is found. Compassion is a state of mind and heart, and while people's opinions vary on what motivates such activism, everyone agrees that it is conducive to effective care.

I remember once sitting between the vice president of the Philippines and the general secretary of the Philippine Council of Evangelical Churches. The vice president had a budget of US$15 million with which to start kindergartens and the general secretary represented an alliance including many of the country's 32,000 churches, many of whom were already involved or interested in kindergarten work. It was an exciting moment.

However, relationships between state bodies and small church-based NGOs are not easy and the Christian community will have to develop ways to engage authorities in frank and meaningful dialogue about how best to develop and maintain the services required.

Many of the philosophical concepts underpinning care and education were developed through the Christian movement and the initial manifestations of these concerns were launched by outstanding men and women of faith. This heritage, combined with the infrastructure of local churches, makes the church a prime candidate for government outsourcing, which, if handled properly, could double the scale of Christian childcare in the century to come.

Essential to the success of this transition is the presence of effective networks serving as brokers between government bodies and smaller church-based NGOs. To be effective, these networks need to operate at local, national and international levels. Some childcare projects are very small and very substandard in terms of quality of care, but through the mediation of a network established to serve their interests, they can offer their services in an appropriate way and be given an opportunity to enhance the work they do.

This can be very successful, as it was in Cordoba, Argentina, where nine service providers got together and formed a network. As a group, they approached the local council and established a partnership whereby the council fitted the bill for most of the goods needed for their work.

Matters don't always run that smoothly. Concerns about interfacing with government bodies are also very real. The danger of becoming dependent on government funds and subsequently being subject to restrictions about what is permissible and what is not is real and not ungrounded. Fears about being closed down overnight as governments change, and fears about being used as cheap propaganda by regimes not worthy of endorsement, stand in the way.

But though government funding should be approached with caution, in many places good relationships with the relevant officials and mediation by network co-ordinators can pre-empt potential problems. Despite the potholes on this path, it has led many to green pastures.

Sustainable fundraising

The development of good relations with government bodies may just sound like more hard work. It may feel easier to continue relying on charitable donations, but these are principally good for the donor and not truly sustainable as a means of reaching children in need. If God is asking the church to reach children in need, he is not giving us three shoes and asking us to put one on each foot. He is giving us a mandate that it is possible to obey. There is a dichotomy, however, between what God seeks to do and the way in which we, so far, have gone about it. As the Western world becomes less generous while more and more needs become apparent, a crisis is evolving. Good work is on the increase, but the money made available for it is declining.

If we are afraid of losing our original vision as we get caught up in business plans to make ends meet, then it is helpful to consider that running a Christian project is very much like running a small business. Christian projects also need accounts, legal status, income and expenditure and so on. Such things seem quite 'unChristian' and boring, but it is time to despiritualize the issue and realize that money and business are spiritual issues. The implementation of practical and professional methods of operation can be endorsed biblically as not just good stewardship, but also plain common sense. Seeing the world from God's perspective makes us bold to do the task in hand and to find other ways of generating income that will help with that.

The world has not gone bust. God has not gone bust. There is as much money now as there always has been, if not more, and we can tap into that source. There are many people with money to spare who can be encouraged to share it generously, as God indeed commands. Yet the fact remains that as a method of long-term funding, donor support alone is ineffectual.

Although change takes time and involves risk and unknown dangers, it is needed. Let's not live in perpetual defeat. Don't forget God is able to do immeasurably more than we could ever dream or imagine.

Bakers and Butchers 7

If you have any encouragement from being united with
Christ, if any comfort from his love, if any fellowship with
the Spirit, if any tenderness and compassion, then make my
joy complete by being like-minded, having the same love,
being one in spirit and purpose. (Philippians 2:1–2)

In a city in Paraguay, children in need were the subject of concern for five local churches. Five churches each ran a soup kitchen. Good news for the children? On Mondays it was because Monday was when each of those churches offered their food. None of them knew about each other. The street kids were feasting on Mondays and starving for the rest of the week.

As I became involved in Christian childcare I soon realized that one thing I did not need more of was meetings. In Nairobi once, a brother from Malawi laughingly explained to me that in Africa Christians often suffered from 'meetingitis'. I assured him that it was not just Africans who had caught the bug, but that the phenomenon was a global one.

I am a committed networker. Five soup kitchens for the same kids on one night of the week is a sad abuse of resources that can be overcome easily if our efforts are co-ordinated. This necessitates some kind of communication and so meetings seem inevitable. I have therefore sought to work out how best to make sure that such meetings actually achieve what is intended, as well as create a sense of trust and fellowship that leads to effective co-operation. The first lesson I learned was to bring together the right people: bakers with bakers and butchers with butchers; that is, people who have a few specifics in common.

Viva Network has sought to develop multiple networks for issues of a local, continental or global nature by bringing together people whose sphere of influence fits into that context. There are also networks of people involved in training childcare workers, people working with sexually exploited children and people working with children at war.

Networks are not about leaving people out, but about ensuring that the right people are talking to each other. My friend Martin is one of the few people I know who become intensely passionate when talking about information dissemination. He compares unwanted information with unwanted goods. You may receive a fantastic pair of pink boots, but if you do not need any boots and you do not like pink, they are no good to you. The same is true of information, which only becomes relevant once it reaches the people who need to know it.

It is only through an active network that information can be passed on to where it is needed. I envisage a one-stop shop in each country for children's projects; a hub of information, a place where both those who have information and those who need information can go; a meeting place with one meeting room for 'bakers' and another for 'butchers', a forum for frontline case workers and another for site administrators.

Once a point of centrality within the Christian childcare community has been established, the task of information sharing becomes infinitely easier. To be effective, such a hub would need to be staffed by 'networkers', a new breed of Christian childcare worker able to serve as diplomats, facilitators and convenors — people like Josefina Gutierrez in the Philippines. A networker would respond quickly and appropriately, sorting information into relevant categories based on their knowledge of the childcare community.

Such channels of information are already in existence and changes are taking place. For example, in that city in Paraguay, street kids now receive food every day of the week. One relevant meeting between the five participating churches not only improved existing efforts for children, it created a model of co-operation for future efforts.

What's the plan?

Most Christian childcare projects develop out of the individual's experience of need and subsequent conviction, courage and capacity to respond. From small and often difficult beginnings projects develop into viable entities, learning as they go along. Occasionally projects grow and multiply to the extent that they become a larger local organization with several projects. A few develop their vision even further and become national or international entities able to plan and evolve as they feel inspired.

Another trend worthy of mention is what I call the newsletter model. Let's take Johnny and Anna (a fictitious couple) who may have a Damascus Road experience which impresses them with the need to work with children at risk. They sell their house, make massive sacrifices, travel to a country where they do not know the language, and set up a project. Lo and behold God is faithful through hell and high water, year after year, and eventually they end up with an orphanage for 24 children in the country of Bandosita.

All the while Johnny and Anna have been writing letters home, expressing the needs of the children at risk they have yet to reach and urging their friends and church to send support to help them push all the open doors they can see around them. 'Please come and help us and please send us money,' they say.

The letters arrive and the church members read them and some of them are inspired to do what Johnny and Anna did, so they move to Bandosita too. They arrive and they all start projects and they all start writing letters home, until suddenly everyone is in Bandosita. Hundreds of Christian projects are sprouting up, caring for hundreds of orphans, while in the neighbouring country of Careros there are no orphanages at all. In fact, there is no ministry to children in need in Careros whatsoever. Johnny and Anna started working with orphans in Bandosita, so everyone else is working with orphans.

The problem is, no one has started to look at the need for after-school clubs. The children in need of these clubs are not orphans, but they have a poor education and so grow up to live in poverty. They cannot read and write, they cannot provide for the families they eventually produce or even keep themselves alive, so their children become orphans in turn, keeping Johnny and Anna and all their friends in business. If Johnny and Anna had started an after-school club, they could have eased the suffering of the children they taught and given them a start in life, which could even have been to the benefit of their future children.

The story of Johnny and Anna is fictional, but it happens in various forms in many places. Lack of contact with existing childcare workers in the target area makes needs analysis difficult and often costly. But without such contact, workers such as Johnny and Anna cannot develop an adequate strategy. It takes an extremely dedicated person to blaze a trail and establish a childcare project, and even then the results are not always what they could be. Sometimes they end up doing more harm than good. What is more, many never even begin for fear of treading into the unknown. Having a strategy not only maximizes the impact of childcare work, it often serves as a catalyst for dealing with as yet unmet needs.

Whether geographically (locally, regionally or globally), topically (for example, street children, children at war) or in terms of performance-related issues (training, accountability, recruitment), a crying need exists for strategic planning of Christian childcare. What's the plan?

We are a community of people who work to help children because of what Christ has done for us and because of what we believe Christ wants to do for children. We may have different organizational tags, flags and mottos, but we are, nonetheless, like-minded. If someone contracts a builder on a big project, the first task he undertakes is to draw up a plan. In the same way, it could be argued that the Lord has contracted us. Where are our blueprints? As I look at current Christian efforts among children in need it troubles me that so much is being done in certain areas or among certain types of children, and little elsewhere. The focus of Christian childcare more often than not tends towards areas where there is a history of Christian engagement with a need and not always to where need actually exists. There is a balance to redress.

Another problem caused by the lack of a common strategy is the partial provision of services. Children may be sponsored by one organization to attend school, but the hygiene in their area is so bad that they suffer from ill health and are rarely able to commit to their studies. Or, a shelter for street children may exist, but there may not be a residential home in place to which they can progress. Specialist organizations benefit children in one way, but leave other areas of importance neglected.

The concept of a one-stop shop, a network for children in need ministries in each country, or globally for specific areas of concern (again, such as street children or children at war), provides an antidote to this problem. Through its forum, the individual strengths of numerous specialist agencies can be harnessed and an overview of who does what and where can be presented to all concerned, ensuring that the Christian childcare community can reach parts not yet reached.

The success of such an initiative will depend on our sense of corporate belonging, on whether we begin to share ownership of the task of childcare, and how much we comprehend our work as obedience to God's mandate. With a willingness to learn from one another we can draw up the blueprints for a job God wants to see completed and has given us the power to do.

'Wisdom in the multitude of counsellors'

Despite significant efforts to help children in need at a grass-roots level, the evangelical movement has made a fairly marginal input into the areas of research and evaluation. Academically and technically we live largely off the experience of others in our thinking about how to shape good childcare practice. This is not for lack of able thinkers, as many outstanding academics, field practitioners and policy-makers belong heart and soul to the evangelical movement but are employed in secular organizations. There they make a vital contribution, but their environment makes it difficult for them to construct and express a Christian response. A 'Christian working in childcare' is ultimately different from 'Christian childcare'. The evangelical community currently offers little opportunity for service for workers of this calibre. Largely grass roots driven, the evangelical movement certainly has the get up and go to do things others may only talk about, but it does not always stop to reflect on and evaluate its efforts. We spend hundreds of millions of pounds and dollars each year on helping children and yet struggle to answer the basic question of 'what works'. Many more serious development and childcare organizations look upon the evangelical movement as energetic and compassionate, but fail to take it into account as a serious entity. Although this has much to do with a low level of awareness of the actual nature and scope of our efforts, it is also partly our own fault and a result of our failure to conduct serious research into practice, policy and performance, and to construct an ongoing platform for serious multi-organizational research programmes. One colleague described our efforts to help children as full of heat but little light.

By co-ordinating our efforts, a network of researchers could be added to our shopping list at the one-stop shop. Beyond the basic question of who does what and where arises the question of the efficacy of our programmes. An analysis of developmental trends of both need and response to need would be a critical tool for strategic planning and could lead to the identification of key models which could be made known throughout the network so that successful strategies could be applied elsewhere.

Such an analysis would seem prudent in any case, but especially given the general lack of resources with which we are trying to respond to an overwhelming need. To a certain extent research and evaluation are always part of any childcare project, but to be more consciously aware of what research is, and how best to structure and utilize it, would be greatly beneficial to many.

Empowering

The Christian movement is one of the largest civic movements on earth today and its congregations worldwide have three things in common. First, they share a heritage of working among children in need that dates back to the early church. Second, they share a faith with those whose current commitment to the requirements of children in need is phenomenal. While children rarely have been the focus of international missions, at a grass-roots level Christian efforts have almost always been substantial. Third, they share a command from God, through the Bible, to care for the needs of others, especially children.

These are three good reasons why the local church should be involved in responding. Sadly, a lot of Christian childcare has been done by parachurch movements. They come to local churches saying, 'Please give us all your best people and all your funds and we will go and do the job.' However, they are now beginning to realize that they are not the ideal platform from which to engage with local needs. Now the local church is coming to the parachurch movements and saying, 'Give us the money and we'll do the job.' Should this happen more and more, a great difference could be made to the effectiveness of Christian childcare today.

In approaching this issue it is important for us to keep in mind the concept of 'sodality and modality'. Dr Ralph Winter is possibly the best-known proponent of this concept[1] which essentially explains the way in which God's people have historically structured their activities.

'Sodality' describes the classic parachurch agency, focused on and committed to a limited range of issues and often comprising a small but dedicated community of highly mobile staff. 'Modality' describes the average local church where the community is more static but has a broader scope of interests and a more permanent relationship with the local community.

This is a useful identification of the wider church's preferred structures of operation, but it should not lead us to underestimate what the local church can achieve. For the truth is that when local churches commit seriously to single issues, their members become, in effect, a 'sodality' and can be highly successful precisely because they are rooted in the local community. What is more, their commitment and achievements can be an inspiration to fellow-members of their church family.

There is tremendous hope in the prospect of mobilizing and enabling the world's 2.3 million[2] local congregations. Local churches have 90 per cent of what it takes to give professional Christian care to children in need. They own buildings, have pulpits from which to mobilize and inspire, and are made up of a network of people scattered across local society and involved in virtually every sphere of public life, including education, business, government and civic duties. Some are rich and some are poor, but they are people who are culturally appropriate, speak the right language, share a commitment to Christ and have the motivation to do his work. Even when we look at this

---

[1] Ralph D. Winter, 'The Two Structures of God's Redemptive Mission' in *Perspectives on the World Christian Movement* (MARC).

[2] Source: Peter Brierley, Christian Research Association, UK.

potential from a secular perspective, and not necessarily through the eyes of Christ, seeing the local church not as an agent of God to bring change, but as a large, able and well-equipped organization, the prospects for the future of Christian childcare look exciting.

It is even more exciting when we do take on board the Christian view of the local church as God's platform for care in the local community, the bearer of the gospel. Research in the town of Crawley found that there were 151 churches in that area. That meant 151 church buildings, with 151 networks of people who no doubt overlapped each other in other spheres of local life, and who were committed to working out the gospel. That model is repeated thousands of times the world over.

Service to the local community is testimony to the gospel of Christ and an active way to draw others to faith. Through such service, relationships can be built with the non-Christian world, as Christian childcare projects form links and make contact with local government and other agencies. Most importantly, the children in need in the community are brought into an environment that is safe and healthy, where they may receive both a good education and spiritual nurture.

I firmly believe that the local church is the way for the kingdom to develop its response to the requirements of children in need. By and large, as we look at Christian childcare we see a huge need to shift it from being a parachurch movement to a movement driven by local people through their local churches. Because many foreign missionaries have come a long way to serve Christ, they tend to be very single minded in their task and they are often, in comparison with local Christians, well trained, on a second career and have money behind them from an overseas network. They have often made phenomenal impact on the cause of children in need and for this we sing praise. But the potential for good childcare in engaging many more local churches and local Christians in bringing a missionary response to their own society is huge.

To do this we will need to develop a new approach from that taken by traditional fully fledged relief and development programmes, as these are often too resource heavy and specialist for a local church to carry out. The relief and development industry can come across as very disempowering to the local church, which is often poor, unskilled and lacking in expertise and money. The programmes we develop with local churches will be more effective if they are carried out not on behalf of our parachurch organizations, but as a local church-owned project with support from external societies. The programmes must be the local church's own project, not a plant from a parachurch movement.

This means losing control and not telling the local church what it should be doing. That is a sacrifice because control is important in charitable work. Without it, it is difficult to achieve all you want to do. If you lose too much control you lose your donors, because you are not doing what they expect you to do, so they put their money elsewhere. The challenge of mobilizing the local church therefore includes the challenge of fundraising and income generation for the purpose of that church's outreach. More often than not, churches in the slums have great compassion but are just as poor as the people they serve. This is actually a strong card, because they are part of the community already. This is where local income generating initiatives can be a great resource, as mentioned earlier, but also where the interplay between parachurch and local church becomes most functional. When a parachurch agency responds to the invitation of a local church to provide advice, resources and contacts, and when that agency encourages local ownership of a project, truly amazing things can happen.

'The Oxford Statement on Children at Risk' says:

> All churches have a responsibility to search for and implement tangible structures by which they can effectively minister to children at risk, both locally and globally. We recommend that they:
> a) make themselves aware of the crisis
> b) make themselves aware of what other people and ministries are currently doing
> c) set aside both financial and people resources in order to link with and participate in specific ministry programmes
> d) regularly pray within the congregational worship service for children at risk
> e) ensure that children at risk and their families are welcomed into and welcome in the church community

f) encourage children to participate in worship and ministry

g) provide a sense of significance, emotional acceptance and support for caregivers.

What would happen if those seven points were adopted by churches worldwide? How wonderful it would be if it started in your own church! Is your church already doing any of those seven points?

People will ultimately do what is important to them. As long as children in need remain an optional extra, broad church involvement with this issue will remain a future hope.

Integrity of witness

I once had lunch with a church planter in Moscow who described work with children in need as of marginal importance. He then went on to explain how poor a reputation most local churches had, how hard it was to encourage meaningful discipleship and to bring home the gospel message. I smiled ruefully to myself as I reflected that he had just highlighted why growing churches should get involved with children in need.

Two of the people on my shelf of heroes are Georgina and Stuart Christine, church planters in Brazil. They went to Brazil solely to set up a church and had little interest in children other than their own. However, as they researched their new community they discovered a need for pre-school and after-school clubs for local children. These poor and often fairly bedraggled kids were invited to come along for a simple snack, a bit of education and a lot of fun. The result was astonishing.

'Our credibility soared and our level of contact with local people was unprecedented,' says Stuart. 'For every child we helped we also touched 30 adults. We didn't have any funding or much idea of how to go about what we were doing, but Georgina constructed a curriculum and we began.'

Georgina adds:

We suddenly had a presence in the community every day of the week and not just on Sundays. Soon we were involved in every aspect of community life and were called on for advice, prayer and practical help. The childcare programme became the first in a long string of community service programmes which we developed as they were requested — programmes such as teaching adults to read, helping pregnant mothers, educational reinforcement and much more.

Eight years after moving to Brazil, more than 1,000 children have been through the Christines' programme and 15 churches have been planted.

'When I came to Sao Paulo I wanted to start churches,' Stuart explains. 'I did, but I realized that the best way to preach the gospel was by meeting people and helping them where they were. The children were the most obvious people to start with, and the result has been staggering.'

Stuart now shares his model with other groups worldwide. His approach is an obvious one, but it would seem that it is still largely ignored by some church planters and agencies. This is more than an opportunity lost — it has an effect on the very credibility of Christian witness. Piedad, a Pentecostal organization in Latin America, realized this and were able to turn around the poor success of their church plant once they opened a school. Through it they won the trust and friendship of local people, and their church grew.

A holistic response to local needs is the loudest way of saying that we care. Discipleship only becomes meaningful when it leads to service. God gave every man and woman the inherent ability to care for children, and childcare provides an obvious entry point to holistic ministry for a local church. What is more pertinent than hungry, hurting children dying on our doorsteps? How can we preach a loving God if we leave these children without a family? As an African proverb states, 'A hungry stomach has no ears.'

It is worth noting that as we respond to the needs of children we will increasingly be exposed to the magnitude of the problems they face. Children in need comprise one of modern-day mission's greatest challenges, but also one of its greatest opportunites.

I met once with the general secretary of the Danish Missionary Council. His name is Birger and I found him in many ways to be a kindred spirit: a restless sort of man, eager to cut through the small talk and get on with business. In talking of Christian work he repeated impatiently, as though to himself, '*Det skal vaere noget godt handvaerk*,' which, roughly translated, is Danish for, 'It must be done well; it must be of good tradesman's quality.' *Handvaerk* means literally 'the work of your hands'. In Denmark, where I am from, your *handvaerk* is a traditional source of great pride and something over which you take great care. It speaks of you more loudly than words.

Christian work with children in need must always be good *handvaerk*, because what we do speaks louder than words — not only about us, but also about our Master, Jesus Christ.

Gaining a Vision for Networking   **8**

Christ is faithful as a son over God's house. And we are his house, if we hold on to our courage and the hope of which we boast. (Hebrews 3:6)

None of my tactics worked with this girl. She wouldn't listen to 'I've given you a swing' or 'I have to wrestle with the others now'. She was about five years old and wore a white dress with big brown spots. It was an awful dress, but she was cute. Her eyes were about the size of saucers. However dark it was in the park, I could see them shining from a distance. Then there was her giggle. She laughed the whole time. You could tell when Anna had arrived at the park because you could hear her laugh despite the noise from the cars honking their horns, and the loud music from the bars.

Anna took to me. When she saw me, she used to cry, 'Patrick!' and shoot across the park to me and level me completely as she landed in my arms. She would smile and hug my knee and ask for more soup, and I would say, 'Oh, well...' and give her some more. When I was giving the children swings, I kept finding her at the front of the queue until she couldn't stand any more. It was great to get to know Anna, because being a street child she was still just a child. Careless of the world and of tomorrow, she enjoyed every minute of her time with our little street team there in Parque Arenal in the city centre of Santa Cruz.

However, at about midnight we would pile into our jeep and go home to our comfortable base. As we went back to feed the children week after week, we found ourselves asking, 'Where's Juan?' or, 'What happened to Juliana?' We lost children one after one. The others would say, 'Oh, they're in the police camp'. The prisons were too full, so when children had done something wrong they went to a police camp. These were indescribably awful places. When the children came back from the camps they were no longer children. Something had broken;

something that needed restoring but was so difficult to put back into them.

I do not know what happened to Anna. She may have been very lucky and found some form of domestic service, or she may have followed most of the older girls into the human flesh trade of prostitution. The latter being the most likely, Anna would soon contract some sexual disease and become just as hopeless and abused as all the other kids there. There was no alternative for her. There was no one to help her.

All this was far removed from the high hopes I had had of making a difference when, aged 17, I went to Santa Cruz to work with street children. Ours was the only project seeking to reach out meaningfully and holistically to around 3,000 of these children. Although Santa Cruz had been hit by church revival, no one was doing anything for the street children. We were a very committed group of young people from a number of different countries and what we did was certainly passionate, but I realized that what we could do to reach these children went only a very little way to fulfilling God's desires for them. Staff with little medical training and few resources were administering first aid. Resources were lacking. Large quantities of food were needed to feed the children, but the project did not always have enough. This really began to trouble me and I started to take a hard look at what we were doing. Our project was established by the 'ideal' person to set up a ministry. His brother led the local Youth With A Mission ministry in town, which meant that he had connections to many of the local churches. He had two degrees, one in sociology and one in psychology, and he had had ten years' experience as a policeman in London. He also had overseas funding and was well resourced to establish a professional ministry. I was there in the third year of the project and we were still struggling to get it off the ground.

The stark contrast between God's desire to reach these children and the efforts of the evangelical church concerned me. I wondered what it was that blocked God from reaching these children. I started to look at the obstacles facing us and realized that the vast majority were of a very basic nature — questions such as how to start an organization, how to resource it and how to work with very difficult children.

Although basic, these were nonetheless very fundamental issues for a group that had absolutely no contact with any other group working anywhere with children in need, whether Christian or non-Christian. My heart was breaking for the children of the streets. Because of my own experience of losing my father when I was twelve years old, I very much associated with their sense of loss, isolation and loneliness. I grieved for them. Although I saw them daily, I found it hard to believe that children lived on the streets. It just seemed so unrealistic, so outrageous that children were abandoned and left to live on the streets.

As we left the park where we met the children every night, twelve of us would crowd into our tiny jeep, some of us even hanging over the edge. I used to stand on the fender or sit on the spare wheel which hung on the back, holding on for dear life. While we were poor, we were still driving home to safety and comfort, and though there wasn't always much food, there was always something. What was more, I was driving home to friends who knew me and somewhat understood me, and I hated leaving the children on the streets. I remember time and time again wishing I could swap. But I couldn't and there wasn't any point in taking the children home to our base as it wasn't really geared towards helping them. We had no way to help them and this really troubled me.

One night I had a vision from God. I cannot explain it in any other way. From out of nowhere I had a strong impression of God speaking to me in a voice that instilled a great sense of hope. Suddenly I realized that if we in Santa Cruz knew who else was doing this, who could tell us where to find resources, how to get training and staff and so on, if we just had a model to develop alongside, we could be far more specific in our response to the needs of the children. This brought to birth in me the concept of the network.

On this particular night in Parque La Libertad, although I had once again watched the children walk hand in hand back to nowhere after an evening of fun with us, I came away with an enormous sense of hope. Yet this was coupled with a great burden for a network, for I realized that this network was vital not only for what we were trying to do, but for what anyone who was a Christian was trying to do on behalf of children in need. Because if we struggled, most possibly others like us were struggling too.

So I made a commitment to find the network. Obviously this network was not visible enough, because I did not know about it. Nor was it effective enough, because as I did not know of it, I could not make use of it. I decided to look for it and to join it.

I subsequently spent about four years looking for the network, but my motivation came that night in Parque La Libertad in Santa Cruz, where I felt God speak to me and instil in me a great hope about the potential of connecting groups like ours with others and thereby providing support, contacts and resources. I realized that the information and resources were probably there. After all, Christians had been working with this issue for hundreds of years. Surely what we were doing was nothing new; street children were nothing new; the problems faced by a Christian minister responding to these needs were nothing new. Yet without somehow being able to tap into that wealth of information and expertise, it seemed as though we were reinventing the wheel all over again and it seemed as though the precious time and resources we had were not being spent on the children and the outreach, but were being spent on trouble shooting models which perhaps would never work.

When I left Santa Cruz sometime later, I embarked on my great search for the network. I must have written more than 1,000 letters to any organization that had Christian or children in its title. I asked them where this network was. I shared with them my experience of grief, but also my enormous anticipation of God's grace and goodwill towards these children, and his ability to orchestrate a solution through the agency of his church, his people. It seemed inconceivable that a network did not already exist; that a movement with the longest track record of working with children in need and such a strong mandate for unity should not have organized itself. Besides, there was a network for virtually everything. Why should there not be a network for Christian ministries working among children in need?

As I visited different projects and wrote to Christian leaders around the world, I wanted to know where this network was. Who had organized it? How could I join it? I wanted to go and be a volunteer, to somehow be involved in this network, because I knew it was key. Whatever I could do, I would do — whether it meant licking stamps or selling postcards on the streets — because the network, to my mind, was the key to unleashing the potential of hundreds of small projects that exist, are hardworking and compassionately involved, yet lack the integrity and professionalism required for holistic Christian childcare. It seemed to me that we needed to merge the professionalism and longevity of holistic childcare with the enthusiasm and the get up and go of the evangelical movement. In that marriage and its success lay the potential of the church to reach an entire generation.

It was a heady business indeed, and I was very excited as I went along. But as the years went by, I realized to my horror that such a network did not exist or, if it did exist, it was very dysfunctional. I never came across anything that was vaguely reminiscent of a network.

I had decided that part of my research should involve spending more time among projects like ours in Santa Cruz to see if we had been an isolated case in point or if, in fact, our problems were common. So in 1993 I travelled for six months around Mexico and Central America with the aim of creating a directory of ministries to children in need in that part of the world. When I started I had six addresses on a piece of paper — mostly the addresses of large organizations and their headquarters. They were all I knew. My Spanish was far from perfect and I had very little money to travel with, so I rode on a Mexican bus from Houston in Texas to Monterrey in the north of Mexico. Arriving very early in the morning, I prayed, almost in jest, 'Lord, it would be very nice if you could provide me a place to stay with a view of the mountains and where my host family have to leave for a prior engagement and I can spend all night praying and collecting my thoughts.'

As I went to different places in the city to research, including the Catholic cathedral and the Christian bookshop, I came across several projects. When I went to visit one of them, the project worker invited me home. His family had an upstairs flat. They explained that unfortunately they had to leave that evening, so off they went, leaving me with a view of the mountains and some spare food. It was amazing, but from that day onwards through eight different countries and 17 cities, as I travelled 15,000 miles and visited about 75 different Christian childcare projects, God provided me with a place to sleep every single night. My daily budget then was $10 and it had to cover all my expenses, food, travel and accommodation. It was not enough for me to stay alive on, but I did, as God provided each day. It was truly quite amazing how I found free lodgings every single night without fail, mostly with people whom I had never met. Travelling by foot or public transport, I would arrive at a new city and enquire about projects. Then I would turn up and offer to wash dishes, stuff envelopes or meet any other need, just so that I could have the privilege of gaining a perspective on the overall condition of Christian work with children in need.

As I visited these projects, I sensed a confirmation of God's grace and desire to do something for these children. Project workers with so little did so much, and even with all the flaws and problems of the Christian movement, these people were still battling on and trying to do what they could. It was a remarkable testimony to God's grace and glory, and I was very privileged to visit these projects.

Yet I also recognized vividly all the same issues that we had struggled with in Santa Cruz. What I discovered both shocked me and confirmed my fears. Many projects were working valiantly (as they had in Bolivia) to rescue the children in their communities, but often with massive debt hanging over them, limited staff to care for the children, and minimal resources to draw from. Even more shocking was the prevalent belief among project leaders that they were the only Christians in their city or region working with such children, though in fact this was usually not the case. On one occasion, I brought together five project leaders in an ice cream parlour, and asked them to introduce themselves to each other. Each one began by describing himself as the only Christian working with children in that area, though by the end of the meeting it had become quite apparent that they most definitely were not.

On another occasion I met some church leaders who had been given responsibility for two orphanages. With no idea how to run these orphanages, they soon had to close them down — a move that caused them to suffer a loss of credibility in the city. At the same time, Christians with vital ministries to children in that city were lacking places to house the children. To make matters worse, one of the best residential childcare centres known to me, a home run by Mennonites, is to be found in that very same city. If only these Christians had been in communication with these church leaders, and had had a high enough profile to be recognized, this disaster could have been averted. Through networking, the church leaders could have shared their community influence and property with the people already motivated and skilled to work with the children.

I was also saddened by the lack of prayer support experienced by many struggling ministries. Local churches may have initially given their blessing to the work that a particular member had felt called to, but apart from occasional gifts of money, the workers were weighed down by heavy responsibilities and challenges, and often felt totally isolated. Their initial vision of spiritual input into the children's lives had been lost in a desperate struggle just to survive.

I remember that, as I was praying one night, a stark comparison was drawn in my mind between the projects I was visiting and the frontlines of the First World War. The only difference was that on this frontline the 'soldiers' were not just covered in mud but were also out of ammunition. Their supply lines had been cut off and there were tensions and problems in many different areas. Heroic people doing heroic work seemed to be abandoned by those who should have supported them and there was a tension created by distant donors who wanted to give money yet kept checks and balances, impatiently expecting to see the world changed overnight by the simple means of a cheque. I encountered project workers who had burned out in their efforts to respond to the needs of children and were now so disillusioned that the only promise they could make was 'never again'.

All in all, it was an amazing trip walking closely with an amazing God. A meeting with the Panamanian Evangelical Alliance on the final leg of my tour spoke to me with particular clarity. Panama is the smallest country in Latin America. During my time of research it had a population of 2.2 million people, half of whom were children and of those half were children in need. When I visited the head of the evangelical church in Panama he did not need me to convince him that his country faced a huge problem where children in need were concerned. He said that there were 1,400 member churches in the alliance, and he guaranteed that 10 per cent of them would get up and do something tomorrow if they had access to the necessary resources, know-how and personnel.

This demonstrated to me the massive potential in mobilizing the churches to meaningful response. Churches are local, they are contextual, they often have buildings and they would love to do something. Yet how? I remember walking, on my last Saturday of that six-month haul, exhausted to the bone, saying to the Lord that it would be wonderful if we could start a network in that country and mobilize maybe 40 churches over 10 or 15 years to reach out to these children. What an enormous response there would be. Even better, that response would not just come from a Western agency, but from the local church. I realized that if we could do that, it would be a far more holistic way of working than simply setting up our own organizations.

I then went home to Denmark, where I decided that I needed to visit the organizations that largely supported these groups in the field. Most of these had headquarters in London, so I took a boat to England. As we approached the white cliffs of Dover I realized that this was a greater step of faith than I had ever taken before, because I did not even know where these organizations were. I had to find out who was the right person to speak to, and I did not know how I was going to do that. All I knew was that to meet Christian leaders at that level at times requires a small act of God if you are a no-one from nowhere, as I was. I needed God to move. I looked at the famous white cliffs with a sense of anticipation as to what God would do.

A week or so later, through God's goodness, I had managed to meet with key people in World Vision, the Salvation Army, Youth With A Mission and Tear Fund. I repeated my story and they all agreed that networking was a key need and they all repeated issues I had come to be familiar with from my research and which highlighted the need for networking at global, organizational and project level. Big organizations like these needed to talk to each other about these issues and find a neutral platform on which to engage and share ideas and so on.

I went home to Denmark, to a little wooden wagon I had standing in a Christian community. There, with a fire crackling behind me, the rain lashing against my windows, I spent most of the autumn in study and prayer. I hid from the world for about three months, contemplating the way ahead. This was a time of sincere prayer, and I emerged with three fairly clear conclusions.

First of all, I resigned myself to the fact that there was no network. Second, I could not deny the overwhelming need for a network. Perhaps one of the single greatest needs in the Christian childcare community was that of a network — a visible and functional network. At all levels this was something that tripped people up, that caused people to duplicate efforts and waste precious resources. Third, I recognized that people across the board were recommending that I pioneer this network. 'This is so overdue, we haven't got time to wait and wait and wait,' they had said, suggesting that I start and see how far I could get.

So I made a commitment before God, in my little wagon near Sminge Lake, that I would do my level best to pursue this. It was something of a sacramental moment, a very special time of committing to God and his will, and trusting him for the knowledge, the wisdom, the resources and the perseverance to carry out the vision that everyone everywhere seemed to agree was greatly needed.

I went back to England, and in February 1994 I met with representatives of all the organizations I had spoken with and reconfirmed the direction I was set upon. I was asked to raise my own support as a missionary because they believed that that would give me greater flexibility, and they were not wrong. Being funded organizationally in the early days would have been prohibitive to growth and difficult to maintain. They also suggested that I move to England and establish a communications centre.

That suited me fine as I had an important reason for wanting to be based in England, and in particular Oxford: a reason called Emily Rose. I met Emily in Santa Cruz where she was working as a volunteer at a missionary orphanage. She came with me to the streets once or twice and we became good friends. When we left Bolivia we kept in touch by mail and I soon realized that I would like to spend more time with her, even the rest of my life. By the time I moved to Oxford we were engaged to be married.

Before moving, however, I returned to Denmark to raise support for the new venture that was to become Viva Network. When I moved to Oxford in May I found a room in an international student community house in the city centre. I set about organizing an international conference on networking to be held in Miami, an idea resulting from my meetings earlier in the year. Those were unforgettable days. In the run up to my cross-cultural wedding to be held in July, I lived and worked in a tiny room with a telephone for incoming calls on the ground floor and a shared telephone for outgoing calls three floors up. My equipment consisted of one old Apple Mac LC with its inkjet printer. The fact that I owned neither a fax machine nor a tie did not seem to trouble the Lord much. Within ten days of my arrival, 18 people had in some way felt a call to participate in the work of Viva Network. Among them was Martin Hull, who immediately and with enormous success began the task of categorizing and analysing information. I vividly remember staggering across Christchurch Meadows in our tired early morning stupor, yearning for good coffee and talking about river mist, church history and data analysis. A deep friendship was forming.

This flood of interest was partly due to the fact that through another remarkable series of events I was introduced to a large group of students at a key student meeting.

In July 1994 Emily and I were married. It was one of those perfect days where everything in the whole world seemed just right. We had a lot to celebrate at this successful juncture of our journey from Bolivia to our wedding reception on this sunny day in Oxford. It had been a long and adventurous trek and we were glad we could continue it together. However, Oxford is atrocious for accommodation at the best of times, and for people with no money it is virtually impossible. We had been content with Magdalen College's weary promise of a single room. But then to our horror that fell through as well and it looked like I wouldn't only be working for homeless children but would be homeless myself! With all doors closed God momentarily appeared to be very far away. We prayed, and mysteriously Emily found herself summoned to a meeting with the chief accommodation officer who apologetically explained that they had had to transfer her onto the graduate accommodation list as opposed to the undergraduate one she was currently on. The implications of this were that we had the choice of two small flats near the Cherwell River and Magdalen Bridge which in the eyes of this officer obviously wouldn't compare to the single room we previously had been offered. We were ecstatic and ended up in an old tumbledown flat threatening to collapse at any minute, but with roof beams and a little fireplace. We loved it!

From here Emily embarked on the final year of her undergraduate degree and I set about establishing an office in the flat, which for sev-

eral months became a centre for research, consultation, and corre-
spondence with churches, ministries and mission leaders the world
over. Living there was a bit like living in a train station. Students from
all over Oxford came and went freely and often stayed for meals. It
was a place of intense discussion, deep prayer, very late nights and
early morning walks; of great joy and deep sadness; of questions and
solutions, food fights, pillow fights, water fights and a whole lot of
fun. I remember my first 'in-office-meeting' with the director of a
major European organization. He had flown to Heathrow for the day
and I picked him up in our 17-year-old Ford Fiesta and took him to
'the office'. As we entered the kitchen we found Emily on the floor
with a multitude of little bottles full of biological samples for her studies spread all over the place. It was indeed a time of small beginnings,
but a time not to be despised.

Not far into the autumn we were joined by Katharine Miles, who now
co-ordinates the Latin American networks. Although Emily and Martin
were not then full-time staff members, they became an influential think
tank for network development and would drive Katharine and me up
the wall with the unavoidable logic of their analyses. Martin began setting up a database containing information about children in need
around the world and soon joined full time. We also had the help of
supporters in Denmark who had been experimenting with the concept
of a network by twinning with Latin American churches. Many of our
Danish supporters left for the mission field in Latin America themselves
as they learned more about the needs there, and the development of a
Danish network taught us many valuable lessons for the future.

The Miami conference was held in October 1994 and as a result an
interim steering committee was established that would oversee the
initial stages of the development of a network. More than anything,
this was a time of confirmation for the vision; a time to evaluate where
we had come to after four years of research and to find the way ahead
for networking. This conference made us aware that a further conference was needed for grass-roots groups. It was important to understand their perspective and facilitate a forum that could engage with
their needs. Katharine became a key person in the development of
this new direction. With the generous support of Latin America Mission and a large dose of her own resources, she succeeded in bringing

this second conference to pass just four months later. In February 1995, Martin, Katharine and I joined the Latin America consultation which took place in Costa Rica, and witnessed the embryonic beginnings of networks in several Latin American countries.

Networks began to spread all over Central and South America, so much so that by September 1997 a regional centre was established in Miami in partnership with Latin America Mission. At this point 16 national networks existed throughout Latin America, but much remained to be done.

Meanwhile, the vision for improving and expanding Christian childcare through networking was growing around the world and Viva Network soon became a hub for evangelicals interested in the concept of networking worldwide.

In August 1995 an investigative conference was held in Ghana, and in April 1997 a co-ordinators conference was held in the South Cone of South America. Following this, a consultation on children at risk was held in Hyderabad (India) in August 1997, and in 1998 an investigation was conducted into networking in South Africa, resulting in a network being initiated there. In August 1998 a conference was called in Bangkok, which 53 delegates from 17 countries in Asia attended. In October a meeting was held in Chicago to launch a network for the United States, and in November the Philippine Council of Evangelical Churches called a conference, which was attended by 73 participants representing 39 Christian churches, mission agencies and service organizations. A network was initiated. In June 1999 a regional network of pan-African leaders began forming as part of a process dating back to March 1997. Later that year networks were formed in both Russia (under the initiative of Russian Ministries) and in the United Kingdom (under the initiative of CARE [Christian Action Research and Education] and the Evangelical Alliance).

The UK network was established in recognition of the fact that UK ministries can suffer just as easily from isolation and fatigue as ministries in other countries. A feature of the UK network is a telephone service, Childlink, run by CARE, which operates on behalf of those who want to help children in need but require more information on how to go about it and who to talk to.

As awareness of the problems faced by children in the United Kingdom increases among the general public, through surveys carried out
by children's organizations and through television documentaries,
individuals are rising in response. Thanks to a series of programmes
on homeless children shown on Channel 4 in the autumn of 1999,
one lady contacted Viva Network's International Co-ordination Office (ICO) asking for help. Appalled by the revelation of dire needs for
shelter beds for a certain age group of children on the streets, she had
determined to set up a shelter as an outreach from her church in
Brighton. At the ICO we were able to put her on to Childlink for the
information and contacts she needed to set about her task.

Alongside all this activity, Viva Network was also gaining a higher profile among international organizations. Positive dialogue was carried
out with major organizations such as World Evangelical Fellowship,
AD2000 & Beyond, and the Lausanne Fellowship. On 1 January 1996
Viva Network initiated the first Worldwide Day of Prayer, for which
information packs were distributed to all members of the network,
and by which a bi-monthly prayer diary was launched. In January 1997
an international consultation was held in Oxford, which was attended
by 51 representatives of 38 ministries, and which produced the 'Oxford Statement on Children at Risk', a document outlining the current state of children at risk globally and what the church's response
to this crisis should be.

This laid the groundwork for Viva Network's Cutting Edge Conference
held in Ashburnham, East Sussex, in the summer of 1998, which
brought together 140 delegates representing work in 171 countries
and launched a new international commission on children in need
called the Council of International Children's Ministries (CICM).
Through such a body as this, it is hoped that Christian ministries will
be able to voice their concerns with enough authority and integrity
to raise the profile of Christian work among secular organizations such
as UNICEF, WHO, ILO and World Bank.

Meanwhile in Oxford, home of what has become known as the International Co-ordination Office (ICO), staff have moved several times
since the first prayer meetings in our flat near Magdalen Bridge. The
volunteer staff has grown in number and the ministry has developed.
Viva Network has been granted legal status and is a registered charity.

It is unbelievable to us how far and how fast Viva Network has come in the space of a few years, but this is testimony both to the grace of God and to the great need for a network among children in need ministries.

How the network works

The high point of a weekend retreat organized for children's ministry workers in Peru best illuminates our mission. The retreat culminated in a worship service on a beach, in which leaders from every project were given a lit torch. Starting with the longest-serving ministry, they each proceeded to place this torch in a big map of Peru made out of sand. Soon the map of the whole country was ablaze and everyone felt a surge of passion for their work as they could see how God was using all of them to reach the whole country. They then signed a declaration expressing their commitment to reach all of the children in need in Peru for Christ.

Viva Network seeks to network among national and local organizations. In many cases, concerns about children in need will be only one aspect, and perhaps not the major concern, of an organization whose primary concern may be evangelism, social welfare or development. Yet the support of all related organizations is vital and exemplifies the principle of one body with many parts. In all of these links, Viva Network seeks to act as a neutral, non-partisan platform for all Christian ministry, with the ultimate goal being more ministry and more effective ministry to children everywhere. The networks we are part of catalysing are autonomous and independent, they govern and resource themselves, but eventually — once developed — affiliate to Viva Network and thus become part of the 'family of credible networks' that constitute Viva Network. We are essentially a network of networks. Member networks have different names and different priorities, but every one shares three things.

First of all we subscribe to the Lausanne Covenant. This is an evangelical statement of faith written in 1974 at a meeting hosted by Billy Graham. This is also Viva Network's value or basis of faith. We are evangelical, or Bible-believing Christians and we feel that we can best define that by the Lausanne Covenant and its elaboration in the form of the Manila Manifesto (1989).

The second thing is an unambiguous focus on children in need. Although many of our members are involved in other fields of endeavour, the part or aspect of their work that has to do with children in need is what connects to the network.

Third is our common identity in the form of a logo. Essential to all our endeavour is a keen sense of community among Christians involved in this field of work. A rallying point in the form of a visible and broadly known and understood network is key to developing a global one-stop shop for Christian ministry to children in need. It communicates a belonging to a bigger and wider picture and some networks are working out ways in which the logo can become a mark of approval for projects that participate in the network and have a certain standard of operation and performance.

Viva Network could be called the International Association of Evangelical Work Among Children in Need, and our aim is to link Christians working with children in need around the world. We do that in three different ways.

First of all, we are a forum, a level playing field, a place where people can meet, share, talk, build communication, co-ordination and co-operation.

Second, in many parts of the world the networks become a representative voice to the church, as they raise the issue of children in need; to each other, as they remind each other of the standards they have to meet; and to the world, as they demonstrate the vast amount of work the church is doing in this area. Further, the evangelical movement is today one of the largest service providers of care, education and welfare, yet little evidence exists of a voice of advocacy at grass roots. We hope to be part of facilitating the evangelical movement to become a formative force in all areas of childcare-related public policy, defending and introducing biblical standards in care and legislation.

Third, we have developed a number of services. Wherever there is an itch, we try to scratch. For example, if a service provider already exists in the areas of, say, engineering or medicine, we act as a referral point to those seeking such services. Where it becomes apparent that no appropriate service exists to meet a particular need, we work with relevant groups to figure out a response and even help them to develop a new arm of ministry if necessary. Certain services can only succeed within the context of a network and they depend on the input and use of several partners. Our main concern is to help groups work together to improve the quality and efficiency of their own ministries. We have developed a prayer diary, a journal, a resource directory, a curriculum and a job centre, as well as many different local services. In Addis Ababa in Ethiopia, children's ministry workers reckon they can probably hire a national co-ordinator on the savings gained from bulk purchases of rice. By purchasing together we can negotiate better deals. It is that simple. We can develop a journal, an annual conference, training events, a co-ordinated approach in our enquiries to the government. We can simply do more.

It is Viva Network's aim to encourage the development of one-stop shops (or networks) for ministries to children in need. Currently 26 networks are at various stages of development in Africa, Latin America, North America, Asia and Europe.

Ingredients of a successful network

Networks begin because people have a shared interest or goal, like mums getting together at the school gate — their children being their shared interest. Relationships deepen as people get together and converse, and trust is established. As mums wait for their children day after day and talk together, they grow closer. In time they begin to share lifts from school and babysitting. In time the network begins to see the advantages of working together to achieve more.

And so we see that ownership is the first ingredient of a successful network. Just as the mums at the school gate have an innate concern for their children's welfare, which leads them to initiate activity among themselves, so local projects must own the need for a network; they must decide for themselves to work together.

Second, the identity of the network must be established and its members be firm in their focus. This means deciding which areas they feel called to and able to target. There is a great range of need in the world, but a band of people can only do what a band of people can do and so a network needs to say, 'We're not about everything, we're just about this.'

Third, networks do not happen without people. If networking just becomes another layer on top of everything else we do, just another burden on our shoulders, then it might as well not happen. For a network to be successful, each member's name should be known, each member's needs should be known. But are network members going to know everything about everyone at all times? I have never seen it happen. The only alternative is to have staff who provide an operation that does the networking for the project workers. I call these networkers or network staff.

Once you have a national networker, or co-ordinator, a problem arises. This person is doing a unique kind of work and one that is no easy task. Groups like Interdev and others have gone to great lengths to prepare network facilitators or co-ordinators, since they realize that the quality of the facilitator can often determine the effectiveness of the network. A real need exists for encouraging, equipping and, to a certain extent, resourcing local facilitators. Viva Network seeks to provide this service for the evangelical childcare community. It is rapidly becoming a 'network for networks', acting as a catalyst for new networks, equipping key networkers and connecting them with other like-minded networks.

On the last night that Jesus spent with his disciples, he did the unthinkable. With a towel wrapped around his waist, he bent down to wash their dusty feet. In this and in his whole life he showed us the true meaning of the word 'ministry': to serve others, even in the lowliest capacity. Around the world we see many Christian groups devoted to serving the weakest and most vulnerable people: children. Viva Network was founded in part to minister to those ministers — to serve those who are serving the needy children of our world.

Are you shocked and disturbed about the nature of God's call upon the church and the challenge facing the Christian community? Have you somehow arrived at that crossroads? Have you somehow come to the point where you say, 'God, we need to change something or we dare not approach your throne, as we simply can't say sorry about things we never even tried to do something about'? Have you seen some of these needs in your own world, in your own work, and have you realized the incredible opportunity we have to help these children? The weight of justice is not something I find many contemporary Christians contemplating, but the word says that to those whom much is given, much is also required. We — the body of Christ — have the capacity, and certainly the command, to get and stay Christ-centred, to pursue excellence, to get organized, to get and networked! It is within our grasp to develop a functional and vibrant network in every location, to respond corporately, to act in unity, to work with integrity and thus transform and expand Christian childcare like perhaps nothing else. The record is clear: so long as you have Christians and children in need in the same place there *will* be a response. Someone, somewhere will be doing something to respond. However, the nature and the quality of that response depends on our ability to respond together. We need to do more than simply respond. We need to respond well.

Viva Network in Action   9

*The God of heaven will give us success. We his servants will
start rebuilding. (Nehemiah 2:20)*

The nerve centre of Viva Network is VivaNet, its database application.
Information can be added or accessed from any computer terminal
authorized to hold the database, which means that when I am travelling, researching children in need ministries, I or any other authorized user can access any new name and address at VivaNet simulta-
neously to everybody's benefit. In this way Viva Network has been
able to make use of every bit of information on contacts to build up a
database on Christian children's projects all around the world.

No global initiative today can operate without information technology
and good information management. At Viva Network we deal with thousands of childcare projects working with hundreds of thousands of children, each project unique in its approach and needs. In our service to
support those who have committed their lives to children in need, accurate information is essential. If we are to raise awareness of projects,
we need to know who they are and where they are. If we are to help
with training, we need to know the type of work they are undertaking.
If we are to help with staff recruitment, we need to be able to match the
skills of staff with the needs of individual projects. If we are to channel
resources, we need to know who is in need of what and who might be
able to provide. If we are to be advocates with the government on behalf of children in need, we have to know how many workers and how
many children we are representing. It is too easy to expect such information to be there when we need it, without questioning how the information may be collected, stored and accessed.

The VivaNet project is a strategic initiative to make this information
available to those who most need it through specially designed database systems in key places around the world. Using it, it is possible to
identify ministries operating in the same locality, or which aim to help
the same types of vulnerable children, for example street children, in

similar ways. The provision of such information is particularly helpful for those planning to start new childcare projects. Existing ministries can be researched to obtain an accurate overview of what ground is already covered. Plans for the new project can then be made in consultation with existing projects in the same area to ensure that ministry is strategic, supported and professionally implemented.

Information on VivaNet is obviously of a sensitive nature and is given out only in accordance with relevant data protection and child protection policies. References are always required before contact details of projects are released to new enquirers and PO Box addresses are always given in preference to street addresses.

Viva Map

VivaNet is just one way in which Viva Network has begun its service of networking children in need ministries. Another initiative is the development of the website http://www.viva.org, which aims to make much useful information about worldwide Christian childcare easily accessible, and which could act increasingly as a forum for the exchange of information. It offers information on children in need and networks of children's projects around the world, on services and resources available, and on how others can participate in meeting needs.

One key feature of the website is a global map on which browsers can click on geographical areas to find out about Christian childcare in the region that interests them: the kind of problems faced by children, information on local projects and childcare services available. Links to the websites of other groups operating in the same area are planned.

Meeting those who share specific concerns, not just geographical location, is also possible on the website by visiting the topical forum pages. These give information on commissions with a specific focus, such as street children or children at war. The development of chat rooms that allow for direct sharing of information means that the website is an excellent place for making contacts. Since it is accessible from all over the world, it is an exciting and dynamic forum for keeping the global Christian childcare community in touch.

Both VivaNet and the information on the website demonstrate to childcare workers in the field who is working in a similar way to them and where. The forging of such contacts allows ideas and even re-sources to be shared across the globe. It is also an invaluable means of gaining prayer support and sharing fellowship with childcare colleagues worldwide.

National and local networks

The key function of Viva Network is to enable childcare workers to network. Tools such as VivaNet and Viva Map assist us in this task, but we are often asked, 'How do I start a network in my area?'

A lot depends on the current level of contact enjoyed by your colleagues in the childcare community locally. The first stage in forming a network is to research who is doing what and how willing they would be to link up with each other. It is only then that relationships can begin to be formed. Viva Network has usually found that a conference or meeting of all interested parties can result in the formation of a network and that in the process of researching and bringing together, potential network co-ordinators come forward.

In forming a new network it is important to remember that you are not alone! It is the Viva Network's International Co-ordination Office's role to assist in the development and support of new networks. The office can help with both research and relationship building. It can also be a source of moral support. For more guidance on forming a network see Appendix 4.

At a national level, here are some of the differences being part of a network can make.

Ghana

In 1995 a conference was organized on behalf of Viva Network by a local group known as Remember the Poor. General enthusiasm for a network was expressed at the conference and a co-ordinator emerged in the person of Emmanuel Dei-Tumi, himself from a difficult background and now the director of Foundation for Future Leaders, an organization involved in placing street children with families.

The conference brought together groups of childcare workers who had previously had little or no contact with one another and brought to light areas of need such as the lack of transport facilities. Alone, projects could not muster funds to provide a form of transport. Together, they managed to obtain a vehicle. There had been a lack of volunteers, since no one could volunteer to help projects they had not heard of. Through the network they became known. Where before there had been a lack of resources and ideas sharing, now they all knew each other and could share their resources and ideas, of which there turned out to be a wealth.

Guatemala

In 1993 I visited a range of projects throughout Guatemala. While there I met Sarita Diaz who shared the vision for networking and continued to pray for a network long after I had left the country.

By 1995 a co-ordinator had arisen for Central America, a Bolivian married to an American, called Betty Smith. Betty worked in El Salvador but was researching the possibilities for networking in Guatemala when she too met Sarita, whom I had lost touch with. She took part in local research, and a conference for children's ministries was held in June 1995. This resulted in a network for Guatemala of which Sarita is the secretary. A president was found in the person of Augusto Marroquin. There were some inevitable teething problems involving misunderstandings about what a network was for (i.e. not a funding agency), but eventually the network began to prove fruitful. Joint prayer breakfasts are held by urban missions; truckloads of broccoli, strawberries and milk given to individual projects are shared with others so that the leftovers do not spoil and go to waste; provincial networks have been formed and contact is for ever being made with ministries as yet unaware of the network.

Food can be shared

If a donation of fresh strawberries is too much for your house of children to eat before they go bad in the hot Chilean weather, at least you now know about the food kitchen down the road that will be happy to share some. Or if that food kitchen wants to order a regular supply of milk and has found that it is much cheaper to bulk buy, even though this would provide more than it needs, then it could share the cost of the extra milk with your house.

More children can be reached

Once projects begin to run more efficiently and less frantically through a network, the quality of care given to the children will improve, as staff have more time and energy to devote to the main purpose of their project: raising children in love. Inevitably and eventually, more children will be reached and fewer children will return to their old lives. This happens when resources are shared, as with the milk and the strawberries, and training is made available to equip Christians to share the gospel with children from difficult backgrounds. For example, when Viva Network's Latin America co-ordinator, Katharine Miles, visited a Scripture Union refuge for street children in Peru, she found that staff there had designed a course for training volunteers but that no one had come forward to make use of it. Earlier, during a radio interview, an enthusiastic journalist had spontaneously announced over the air that Katharine would hold a seminar. Honour bound to hold a seminar she had not planned for, Katharine was happily surprised when about 50 people turned up — 50 everyday Christians who lived in the area and had a real heart for working with children. At the end of the seminar the question they were all asking was, 'How can I get trained to work with street children?' The discovery of Scripture Union's programme answered their cry.

In Chile one lady has a home for girls up to the age of 13. Another lady works with prostitutes who are slightly older. When the younger girls were given some clothes that were more suitable for women, they gave them to the older girls.

Information can be shared

In Paraguay a woman who ran a weekly outdoor Bible study in a park, called 'Happy Hour', was increasingly disturbed by the noise and the weather. In fine weather, people were always walking past and in the summer it rained so often that she thought she would have to cancel her Happy Hour for half the year. Viva Network's national co-ordinator got wind of this and remembered that there was a kindergarten in the area which was not used on Saturdays when the Happy Hour took place. She investigated and found that the kindergarten was run by a Christian lady who was more than happy to lend it for the Happy Hour all year round, and eventually got involved with running it herself. Around 50 children now enjoy the study and snack afterwards each week.

This last story shows how crucial it is to have a national network co-ordinator, someone whose ministry is to network, and who therefore has the time and mental space to make helpful connections.

National networks provide a platform for churches to learn about ministry to children in need and are a source of help for new initiatives. This is verified by the experience of Eyiba Yamaria, Viva Network's national co-ordinator for the Democratic Republic of Congo. Eyiba, who runs a Sunday school and plans to build an orphanage, testifies to learning more about how to help children at risk from visiting other projects:

We think networking is the basis of going on with this work, because with a network we can have resources, information and training — especially training. To reach a child is one thing, but to keep on protecting the child is another thing...

> I think networking is the key to the kingdom of God, because one man cannot do everything, but if we are together, many organizations, many churches, many individuals, we can work more effectively.

Childcare workers feel less isolated

As networks develop and the positive consequences multiply, Christian childcare workers begin to feel more motivated and encouraged. Prayer support and friendship are now available to them and they no longer feel isolated. This is one of the biggest fruits of networking. No one who is aware that they are part of a group of people, a family whose members are all doing the same thing, can continue to feel alone. The encouragement that a sense of belonging engenders is empowering beyond measure. We all know how it is. We all know what it is like to feel alone and discouraged while doing a huge task. But if we feel we are part of a greater body in our city or in our nation, and we are all pulling in the same direction with a common purpose, then it seems more manageable somehow.

Unity is encouraged

Where networks are established, God's name is glorified, since unity is promoted. Unity is a testimony to the body of Christ and gives Christian childcare workers a stronger voice in official circles.

Most national networks are co-ordinated by nationals who attempt to raise funds nationally for network activities, such as annual conferences for training, sharing and strategizing, and monthly prayer meetings. Through a national network, information is disseminated among projects. Contacts are made in the media, government lobbying is undertaken, prayer is encouraged and a link is formed with international services. The consolidation of national networks relies on the co-ordinating bodies having the equipment they need, such as computers with databases and email, and fax machines. This way they can interact meaningfully with Viva Network and make the most use of the services on offer.

Both funding and gifts in kind are needed to resource these locally staffed offices around the world.

Influence can be exercised in the secular field

Evidence of the success of national networks in acting as a voice to NGOs and governments is already prevalent. We have already mentioned successful incidents in Cordoba and Nairobi. In Colombia, after the President met with Viva Network co-ordinators, he gave them official recognition and input into the government's social services.

Stephen de Beer of Pretoria Community Ministries in South Africa reports that networking has even helped to develop good relations with the local police. In the past, he says, the police were sometimes guilty of harassing young girl prostitutes, but now several committed Christians are in key management positions in the police force and have been open to positive suggestions made by former prostitutes now in care, through the Community Policing Forum. Police no longer arrest prostitutes on the streets, but instead suggest they make use of a local project.

Another success story in Pretoria involves the local zoo. Run by Christians, it opens its gates to girls from Stephen's project on certain days, for pleasure and for educational purposes. 'Throughout the city there are wonderful networks in place, both with Christian and non-Christian organizations,' Stephen says. 'Many of the non-Christian organizations have brought us in touch with Christians who understand the difference they can make. Somebody called it the human bridges of God. It's great indeed.'

Networks can also work to help each other, as is seen in the south cone of Latin America, where national networks in the region produce a publication together, which raises awareness and keeps members informed.

Prayer diary

The Viva Network prayer diary is a means of generating prayer support for existing ministries around the world and raising awareness of children in need ministries among the church at large. Copies are sent to Viva Network supporters and members four times a year, and they contain prayer requests provided by member ministries. It is immensely encouraging to note the extent to which prayer points published in the diary find an answer. Increasingly, feedback points are featured as a source of praise and encouragement. The number of ministries using the prayer diary is growing, along with the numbers of churches and individuals using this valuable tool. The prayer diary is translated into Spanish by the Costa Rican Viva Network co-ordinators.

Rapid response prayer link

Since the prayer diary is published at fixed times of the year, it does not cater for needs of a more urgent nature. For this reason, a further prayer service has now been established using email. Any urgent prayer requests can be posted this way and passed on at no charge.

Worldwide Day of Prayer

Since 1995 the first Saturday of June each year has been designated as an international day of prayer for children at risk. Childcare workers and supporters all over the world use this day to focus their prayers and to encourage a wide range of people to pray. Prayer mobilizers in each locality have access to a number of different tools provided through the network, including a substantial resource pack full of case studies, information, statistics and prayer points. These can be used in churches or small groups, or by families or individuals praying at home.

I was greatly encouraged once when I sat next to a well-known childcare worker from Sri Lanka at a conference in Canada. In telling me about his work and his various dreams and desires for it, he mentioned a prayer initiative called the Worldwide Day of Prayer for Children at Risk. The year before, he said, evangelicals in his country had marked this day with a prayer march joined by 3,000 people in the capital of Colombo. 'That event alone did more than any other to alert Christians to the needs facing children in my country,' he told me. 'Have you heard of it?' I smiled to myself as I told him that I had and that I was so glad he had found it useful. When I met this man again later, he told me that the Sri Lankan Government had unexpectedly placed the needs of children at risk at the top of its agenda. Prayer precedes power.

The day of prayer involves people, churches and groups who would not otherwise concern themselves with children in need. It is an excellent awareness raiser and varies in format from three old ladies getting together over tea in a Welsh church hall, to 24-hour radio broadcasts in Peru, to mountain prayer vigils in Africa, to young Scandinavians spending a night in a cardboard box on the streets of their cities; not to mention the kind of prayer march featured in Sri Lanka.

Worker and training services

Shortage of workers is a problem for many organizations. Those Christians who choose to get involved often do not know where to turn and how to prepare themselves for ministry. Viva Network seeks to network both personnel and training resources to the places where they are most needed. To this end we have opened a job centre. This is a small-scale operation that matches up ministries' needs with individuals looking for opportunities to serve. It is run on-site at Viva Network's International Co-ordination Office.

Resources Directory

There are many written, audio and training resources about children in need and how to work with them, available from a wide variety of organizations, yet most projects do not know that they exist or how to get hold of them. Viva Network has produced a directory of such resources, informing how much they cost and how to get hold of them. This directory is produced in-house and is personalized to each enquirer. Subscribers are encouraged to pay, but those who cannot are subsidised.

Resources library

Viva Network offices are becoming centres for information and training resources. Collections of useful books and other resources are being built up for the benefit of network members and others who need information but cannot afford to buy all the resources they need.

Journal

Viva Network has developed a journal, *Reaching Children at Risk.* This is a partnership project between several international agencies and contains practical articles and advice for Christians in the field. Contributors are seasoned field workers with expertise in particular areas of ministry to children in need. Each issue focuses on a particular topic, such as administration, conflict and training, and contains sections such as 'Care for Caregivers', 'Training Resources' and a pull-out 'Toolkit', as well as feature articles.

Handbook

Many training services are expensive and hard to get hold of. In response to this, Viva Network is producing a series of low-cost handbooks for network members, containing information on how to get started, based on the experiences of successful projects.

Many Christians working with children in need have years of experience from which they have learned precious lessons. These lessons will be included in our handbooks focusing on different areas of work with children in need. Examples include books on multi-stage street child ministry, tackling child prostitution and provision of vocational training. The handbooks are also designed to encourage others to become involved in the work.

Trainer's Directory

There is a great need to enable experts in the field of mission to children in need to advise and train less experienced groups and individuals. The Trainer's Directory has profiles of carefully selected individuals who have training skills to offer, and will be used to invite suitable people to take part in training services offered through national networks.

Administrative services

Many projects need help to run a smooth administration. Viva Network is developing various services that offer advice and help and that recognize well-run projects. These include the ministry accreditation scheme run by some national networks. Having accreditation helps ministries to raise funds and recruit personnel.

Regional representatives and friends of Viva Network

Viva Network offers the chance to become a regional networker to those excited about what Viva Network can do in their area. Likewise, they could become a friend by committing themselves to donate on a regular basis.

What Viva Network does not do

Viva Network never starts its own childcare projects. This is not our role and would destroy our ability to remain neutral and unbiased. Viva Network is not a fundraising agency, although we would love to see a secretariat for sustainable financing established at some stage soon. This would involve networking financial needs, building capacity among our members to understand their own funding needs, identify potential donors and know how to approach them for what. Viva Network is a constituency-based network organization and faith in Christ is a prerequisite for membership. We readily acknowledge that many non-faith-based groups are doing excellent childcare work and we hope to serve more and more as an effective liaison or bridge to these groups to increase meaningful exchange of information and resources.

The future

We are conscious that our current opportunities far exceed our ability to utilize them. We need to grow. A host of concepts and plans are waiting for God to raise up the right people to develop and maintain them. For instance, in future we plan to develop workshops, create a central pool of training materials and produce a training calendar with details of training for childcare workers worldwide.

We also hope to publish a compilation of articles and chapters of useful books in one volume to save childcare workers both money and time in their own research. To this end we are also considering making bulk purchases of useful books on behalf of members.

But the idea we are most excited about is the worldwide curriculum for the training of Christian childcare workers mentioned in Chapter 5.

We estimate that there are 110,000 Christian childcare workers. Until very recently virtually no training has been made available to them. Other professions have certificates of training and the Christian childcare community no less needs to develop its own international certificate of Christian work with children in need. Over the last four years we have become aware of the enormous need for training as time and again, from across a broad section of the Christian childcare community, we have heard the cry, 'Training is essential if we are to be far more successful and efficient.'

The Christian childcare community is a large community already at work and it is not easy to extract over-stretched staff from their daily work and lock them away in a training institution for months at a time. While certification and standards in training childcare workers are essential for the community, a further need exists to create a pool of training resources that could encourage and facilitate the development of a host of training initiatives for the grass roots. Creativity and flexibility in this task are essential for success. Both certification and on-site training are essential.

We set out to investigate who was providing training at that time. To our dismay after three or four years of research we found that there was virtually nothing in existence and that what there was had a very limited use and was also largely unheard of. We started to share this need with those people whom we had discovered were involved in one way or another and with various key organizations, and found there a strong resonance about the need to develop a training course that would be given the highest credibility.

We put together a workshop with people from key constituencies in July 1998. Present were grass-roots workers who had been in the field for many, many years and knew what a childcare worker needs to know, and Christian academics aware of the need and of what academic institutions require. Over the course of a week, we drank many cups of strong coffee, drew down the blinds, threw away the key, and worked non-stop day and night to produce a draft curriculum. We have now put together the first of four modules, a 40-hour introductory course, of what could become known as the International Certificate of Children at Risk Studies. We left the workshop and found enormous interest among credible academic institutions to pilot the course. Many of them did, including Wheaton College in the USA, Cornerstone College in South Africa and Evangelical Theology Seminary in Croatia. To get so many institutions on board so soon is a move of God and it is encouraging to see how children at risk studies is becoming a new field of academic endeavour. The need is great. Over the next 10 to 15 years, at least a million new childcare workers need to be developed and it would be ideal if they all had the opportunity to hold a certificate that is internationally recognized, comprehensive and professional; and modular, so that they can take one module in one place and another module somewhere else as suits their personal mobility.

Viva Network is also working on a text book for children in need, and is setting up apprenticeship schemes at model programmes for students who want to learn the trade. We are continually looking for model ministries that can train people and send them on.

A trainer index is being developed of specialists in the field, child psychologists, street workers, and others who are willing to give teaching sessions, and a training resources database along the lines of VivaNet is also being considered.

The Vision Continues   *10*

Let us run with perseverance the race marked out for us.
(Hebrews 12:1b)

Across the road from my office is a school. At break times the children make loud, happy noises as they pile out into the playground. Every now and then I allow myself the luxury of leaving the office and walking past this school to remind myself that many children are happy, full of life and energy and worried only about their homework, the damage to a favourite toy or that they have once more kicked their football over the fence and into their grumpy neighbour's garden. I think childhood is supposed to be like that. Childhood should be a time of safety, exploration and growth.

I remember the warm summers of my own childhood, when our entire family went sailing on the beautiful lakes of Silkeborg, my home town in Denmark. There was my mum, with her basket full of amazing foods; my dad, preoccupied with navigating the boat; my brother, trying hard to impress our cousin, whom I think he rather liked; and me, in my orange life-jacket with my oversized hat and blue wellington boots, trying to spot fish or catch insects, worms or anything else that moved. I remember the lazy afternoons in the forest, the boat anchored to the shore of the lake as we sat down to read, relax, debate, eat and swim.

Childhood is precious

I was part of organizing a gathering for senior childcare leaders from across the world and we asked ourselves a foundational question: Why work with children in need? One of the people I most admire, Wesley Stafford, answered it this way:

> Why do we work among them? Any mama or papa here who puts their little children to bed at night knows what they give to us. They give us everything they have. They give us that big, tight hug before they lie down, they give us that little kiss,

they give us those three little squeezes on the hand that say, 'I love you.' They give us their giggles, and they give us their laughter; they give us their smiles, they give us that twinkle in their eye, they give us colourful little bits of paper and string and wood and glue ...

Nobel prizewinner, Gabriella Mistral, put it this way:

We are guilty of many errors and many faults,
> but our worst is abandoning the children, neglecting the fountain of life.

Many of the things we need can wait. The child cannot.

Right now is the time his bones are being formed,
> his blood is being made and his senses are being developed.

To him we cannot answer, 'Tomorrow'. His name is 'Today'.

Life is sacred, life is priceless, and yet despite the inexpressible value of children, they are at great risk, perhaps greater than ever before. We have looked at the statistics, we have heard the stories and we have studied the Christian response. Children's primary enemy is not what we do, but what we fail to do. It is obvious that much is being done and that the potential for doing more is huge. There is a great task ahead!

I believe that Christian outreach to children in need stands at a crossroads. A response to the needs of children at risk from the Christian community is inevitable as people seek to follow Christ. However, if we continue as at present, then our efforts almost certainly will become increasingly peripheral to the overall efforts made in education and childcare.

Privatization of care, welfare and education is a reality. It's happening hand over fist worldwide, and the church — as one of the largest civic infrastructures in the world — stands at the front of the queue for the fall-out. With a history for and current commitment to helping the poor and needy, the church is often seen as an obvious candidate. Officials will pursue privatization not only because it is cheaper, but also because they realize that the increase in population over the next 20 years will mean intense pressure on all caring services. This will not be easy for anyone and it is human nature for people to want to blame someone for their suffering. As this becomes more and more evident, any politician with half a brain will seek to ensure fingers are pointing anywhere but at them. Outsourcing provides that opportunity. Outsourcing is safe. From an economic point of view, institutions like the World Bank are slowly but surely waking up to the fact that even economic growth depends on social stability, good health and good education. If governments can't deliver that, even the Bank must look elsewhere in order to achieve its objective of economic growth.

From Lima to London, from Manila to Manitoba, from Colombia to Chicago the trend is the same, and Christians are offered the opportunity to play a key role in redefining what is known as the 'caring industry' and the educational sector. The stakes are high. There is perhaps nothing the church needs more than real opportunities for meaningful and visible action. After all, 'As the body without the spirit is dead, so faith without deeds is dead' (James 2:26). The conviction of sin that leads to conversion involves nothing less than the spiritual birth of the unbeliever, who moves from darkness into light, from death into life and thus gains status as a citizen of a new community. Along with this comes a new commitment that creates more than an outlet for good intentions, but transforms and empowers those it touches, and in turn transforms others. The road to maturity in Christ must surely involve service, which in turn, through the power of God, transforms the world.

Through networking we can realize and harness our inheritance, our resources and our potential, and thus bring about a massive acceleration of Christian care for children. The starting point for enabling this to happen is a sense of community among Christians working with children in need and visible and functional entry points for all participants in this community through which to meet their appropriate peers. Such networks are essential to the ability of the church to respond in this situation, but networks are not easy to launch. Launching and operating a network is different from almost anything else and the opportunities for making early but fatal mistakes are abundant. That is where a network catalyst like Viva Network becomes highly useful.

It seems to me that Christ provides each generation with specific challenges and opportunities with which to extend his kingdom. These opportunities represent potential turning points for the church and her witness to the world, and I am convinced that the challenge of reaching the multitude of children in need is just such an opportunity. I believe that opportunity is ours to grasp by the power of Christ and his Holy Spirit. If not us, who? If not now, when?

Allow me to elaborate. I often wonder why it took such a long time for the abused labour force of the industrial revolution to formulate a response. The average life span of people in Manchester was under 40 years and their hardships cannot be disputed. Children were working virtually naked in steaming hot or icy cold factories and they were often maimed for life or became terminally ill from the dust and the extreme conditions. Long hours, low pay, poor housing, no education. There was better healthcare for the working horse than for the working man. This unjust pattern was repeated around the world. A hundred years of silence resulted in the formulation of the Marxist manifesto and the subsequent rise of communism and its counter-movement Nazism. A hundred years of global conflict have followed, including some of the worst wars known to humanity — World War Two, Korea, Vietnam and Afghanistan to mention a few. Why was there such a delay in the response?

I have my own theory about this and I dare — with some trepidation — to share it with you. I believe God called upon his people to respond. In the face of great injustice a just God begged his church, his people, for action. But apart from scattered initiatives here and there, we — as a movement — failed to respond. Action was required and once this mandate had been rejected or ignored by the church, the baton was grasped by someone else. With it passed the blessing that could have been ours: the opportunity not merely to execute justice but to glorify Christ — in the lives of the multitudes as well as in society. We lost far more than human lives in those wars. We lost souls by their millions as empty ideologies and all of their paraphernalia were explored with utter futility.

And again, the same story goes for the green movement. Why did it take so long — almost 200 years — for a movement of concern to gain serious momentum? Did God in fact wait with bated breath for someone to take on the mandate, grasp the challenge and fight the battle for good stewardship of resources, for the preservation of his beautiful creation against the needless violation of a lazy consumerist world, driven by hedonism and self-indulgence?

The destruction of nature and the abuse of the work force were an affront to God and I wonder if a challenge from heaven, an opportunity for appropriate action, went forth for decades, even centuries, with no one listening. Did God call out 'Whom shall I send? And who will go for us?' and no one responded? I wonder and I am not sure, but I marvel at the consequences of those lost opportunities. Eventually the baton was taken by the flower power movement of the sixties, which mixed nature with free drugs, free sex and a unique blend of homespun religion focused around the sacred autonomy of the individual. Soon abortion was legalized and in America alone more than 28 million babies paid the price as they were abandoned in abortion. But many more were lost as postmodernity exchanged truth for convenience and responsibility for comfort. Forgive me for theorizing and speculating, but I wonder whether the church was called upon for action and ignored the call for too long.

The evangelical movement stands ideally poised for massive expansion of its outreach to children in need. If we can organize ourselves in functional networks, we can make visible the largest body of care currently in existence and expand it greatly. Out of that, a movement of prayer could mobilize every Christian on earth to intercede for children in need. Out of that, connectedness and higher standards of performance could double or triple the number of children reached with the same resources invested. Out of that more than 10 per cent of the 2.3 million congregations could be mobilized to reach children in need. Out of that could come a concerted effort to raise up a body of approximately a million new workers who could be provided with decent care and training. And out of that, evangelical care for children could be seen and known everywhere as a respected and appreciated force.

The challenge of children in need is as much an opportunity as it is a problem. If tackled well it could provide a multitude of opportunities for service throughout the body. It could — like no other activity — provide credibility for our local and global witness and it could provide a multitude of boys and girls with a sensitive and appropriate introduction to the Father of the fatherless: the high King of heaven, the Ruler of all, the great God who cares for you, for me and for every single child with whom we share this generation.

The Lord wishes to see these children reached. He yearns with a fatherly passion to demonstrate his care for them, and he is calling his church — you and me — to respond with no ifs or buts. God is not just willing, he is able to enable us to make a lasting difference in the lives of children who suffer. There is hope for the children of the world!

It was this belief that inspired those of us who met to pray on Monday mornings near Magdalen Bridge and which led to the development of Viva Network. It is this belief that empowers us to continue developing the network today. Pressing on, we are 'confident of this, that he who began a good work in you will carry it on to completion until the day of Christ Jesus' (Philippians 1:6). Why don't you join us?

Vision Statement   *Appendix 1*

The vision of Viva Network is to improve the quality and increase the quantity of Christian work with children in need, through networking groups engaged in this work.

Aims

The aims of Viva Network are:

- Christ-centredness — to encourage a strong and consistent focus on Christ and his mandate to the church among Christians working with children in need.

- Community — to increase the sense of community between Christian workers.

- Communication — to enable the flow and exchange of information, resources and ideas.

- Commitment to excellence and competence — to provide opportunities for critical analysis and improvement of Christian work among children in need.

- Co-operation — to facilitate increased co-operation and co-ordination between Christians involved in this work.

- Compassion — to mobilize the church worldwide in meaningful ways of meeting the needs of 'children at risk'.

- A Christian platform — to increase the profile of Christian work with needy children within the church and secular bodies, and to facilitate greater co-operation between these two groups.

Core values

Obedience to Christ

Viva Network is compelled by personal and corporate obedience to Christ. This involves demonstrating the gospel in word and deed.

Community

Viva Network seeks to strengthen community in the body of Christ. This involves communication and commitment to meaningful relationships.

Love

Viva Network seeks to encourage love in the body of Christ. This involves sacrifice and servanthood.

Unity

Viva Network promotes unity. This strengthens the voice of Christian outreach to children in need.

Integrity

Viva Network encourages integrity in the body of Christ. This involves honesty, openness and a commitment to accountability.

Sharing

Viva Network promotes sharing within the body of Christ. This involves an attitude of humility and, consequently, the multiplication of efforts.

Commitment to excellence

Viva Network promotes a commitment to excellence in all Christian endeavours. This involves a commitment to change and improvement.

Useful Contacts   *Appendix 2*

For further information on children in need or working with children in need, or to obtain any of the resources mentioned in Chapter 9, please contact:

> Viva Network
> PO Box 633
> Oxford OX2 0XZ
> UK
> Tel: 01865 450800
> Email: info@viva.org
> Website: www.viva.org

The Council of International Children's Ministries (CICM) is the network for international Christian organizations working with children in need. It is affiliated to Viva Network and provides a forum for those organizations who work in more than one country, and major national organizations, to network on global issues and share resources, skills and expertise. It encourages greater professionalism and provides a platform for strategic planning and partnerships between members. It also seeks to promote prayer and advocacy on behalf of 'children at risk'.

If you are interested in making contact with international Christian organizations working with children at risk please contact the CICM Co-ordinator at the address below. You can also visit our website: www.viva.org/cicm or cicm.net where contact details for members of CICM are listed, and you can link to their websites.

> Contact: Deborah De Kock, CICM Co-ordinator
> Viva Network
> POBox 633
> Oxford
> OX2 0XZ
> UK
> Tel: +44 (0) 1865 450800
> Fax: +44 (0) 1865 203567
> Email: ddekock@viva.org / cicm@viva.org

Viva Network regional addresses and contact numbers

The addresses given below are correct at the time of printing. Up-to-date information on network contacts can be found through the Viva Network's international office and on the website at the address above.

AFRICA
Lorenzo Davids
c/o Cape Town City Mission
PO Box 36091
Glosderry
Bridgetown 7702
South Africa
Tel: 27 21 691 9574
Fax: 27 21 691 9598
Email: cmf1@iafrica.com

LATIN AMERICA (overall)
Katharine Miles
c/o Latin America Mission
PO Box 52-7900
Miami
FL 33152-7900
USA
Tel: 1 305 884 5687
Fax: 1 305 885 8649
Email: kmmiles@lam.org

LATIN AMERICA (South Cone)
Fausto and Iris Re
Pio Angulo 850
2550 Bell Ville
Cordoba
Argentina
Tel: 54 5 342 6102
Fax: 54 5 342 8393
Email: TULIO@southlink.com.ar

ASIA
Ian de Villiers
c/o Viva Network
POBox 633
Oxford,
OX2 0XZ
Tel: 01865 450800
Fax: 01865 203567

Local networks

ARGENTINA (Buenos Aires)
Networker: Ana Jorquera
Union Biblica Argentina
Aristobulo del Valle 1447
1638 Vicente Lopez
Buenos Aires
Argentina
Tel/Fax: 54 791 3030
Email: anajor@cristianet.com.ar

BOLIVIA
Networker: Corina Clements
Cajon 3216
Santa Cruz
Bolivia
Tel: 591 3 46 1471
Email: corina@scbbs-bo.com

BRAZIL (MEN)
Networker: Mark Stuckey
MEN-Confederacao
Rua Domingos de Morais 1777
04009-003 – Vila Mariana
Sao Paulo, SP
Brazil

BRAZIL (Rio de Janeiro)
Networker: Teresa Santos
Av.4 – No.1314 – Lote 4 – Qd.25 – Soter

Itaipu – Niteroi – Rio de Janeiro
Brazil – CEP.24342-340
Tel: 55 21 350 8915
Email: belteca@hotmail.com

CHILE (San Diego)
Networkers: Maria Paz Carcamo Hodge and Pamela Romero
La Red Viva de Chile
Sotero del Rio 109
depto. 408
La Florida
Santiago de Chile
Chile
Tel: 562 262 4406
Tel/Fax: 562 696 6459
Fax: 562 542 1015
Email: via Andrea Gutierrez: solsonip@ctcreuna.cl

COLOMBIA
Networkers: Carlos and Nancy Bernal
Apdo. Aereo 016617
Bogota
Colombia
Tel: 571 892 3092
Tel/Fax: 571 269 7787
Email: redviva@col1.telecom.com.co

DEMOCRATIC REPUBLIC OF CONGO
Networker: Ejiba Yampia
Eglise Pentecotiste Des Secouristes
1 Avenue Muaza
Commune de Ngaba
Boite Postale 13461 Kinshasa
R.D.C.
Tel Wk: 243 12 58110
Fax: 243 12 20091

COSTA RICA
Networkers: Roberto and Roxana Grego
Apartado 274-2350

San Francisco de Dos Rios
San Jose
Costa Rica
Tel: 506 219 4022
Fax: 506 219 4550
Email: rgrego@racsa.co.cr or cpcinter@sol.racsa.co.cr

DENMARK
Chairman: Preben Aagren
Halkvej
84 Halk
6100 Haderslev
Denmark
Tel: 45 74 57 17 00
Prayer Co-ordinator: Gerda Rasmussen

FINLAND
Networkers (Finnish only): Paivi and Pentti Matara
PL 82
FIN-28401
Ulvila
Finland
Tel/Fax: 358 2 538 9947
Kari Pekka Murtonen
Kuusitie 17 as 1,
40800 Vaajakoski,
Finland
Tel: 358 14 666647
Email: MurKari@jypoly.fi

GUATEMALA
Networker: Mauricio Rodriquez
Apartado Postal 2171
Cuidad de Guatemala
Guatemala
CA
Tel/Fax: 502 442 0062
Email: famaindust@emailgua.com

HONDURAS
Networkers: Katja and Max Hernandez
Apdo.Postal 3881
Tegucigalpa MDC
Honduras
CA
Tel: 504 239 0789
Email: maxkatja@hondudata.com

MEXICO – BAJA CALIFORNIA
Networker: Daniel Young
PO Box 432172
San Ysidro
CA 92143-2172
USA
Tel/Fax: 1 619 575 8112
Email: danyoung@fastwave.net

NIGERIA
Networkers: Solomon and Mercy Tarfa
PO Box 12558
Sabon Gari
Kano State
Nigeria
Tel: 234 64 633236
Fax: 234 64 644392
Email: wisdom@micro.com.ngjtckano@hyperia.com (put
'Viva' in subject line)

PARAGUAY
Networker: Maria Angelica de Ojeda
Email: fabian@rieder.net.py

PERU
Networkers: Ana Delgado and Luz Sanchez de Rojas
La Red Viva Peru
Avenida Guzman Blanco 465
Departmento 301, Oficina 4
Lima 1
Peru

Tel: 51 1 330 5365
Fax: 51 1 427 4923 (Att: Red Viva)
Email: red_viva@lima.business.com.pe

PHILIPPINES
Networker: Josefina Gutierrez
PO Box 4194 MCPO
1281 Makati City
Philippines
Tel/Fax: 63 2 8100095
Email: jogutz@hotmail.com

SLOVAKIA
Networker: Miss Ursy BottingLiscie Nivy 12,
821 08 Bratislava
Slovakia
Tel: 421 7/555 71 037 (home)
Email: ubotting@compuserve.com

SPAIN
Networker: Enrique del Arbol
Apdo 21093
Madrid 28080
Spain
Tel/Fax: 421 7 525 9859
Email: dignidad.org@mx3.redestb.es

SOUTH AFRICA
Networker: Karen Hinder (Arise)
c/o Thembalitsha
PO Box 275
Rondebosch
Cape Town 7700
South Africa
Tel: 27 21 685 1656
Fax: 27 21 686 9320
Email: arise@nis.za or arise@ilink.co.za

URUGUAY
Networker: Kurt Duck
Hogar de Ancianos
Ecilda Paullier
San Jose
C.P. 80.002
Uruguay
Tel: 598 349 2066
Fax: 598 349 2148 Ext: 2066

USA
Networker: Michelle Butler
504 East Lexington
S. Carolina 29072
Tel: 1 803 957 6101
Email: rev2123@aol.com

Miami Networker: Rich Sawyer
c/o Latin America Mission
PO Box 52-7900
Miami
FL 33152-7900
USA
Tel: 1 305 885 8649
Email: sawyer24@gate.net

VENEZUELA
Contact: Hugo Castro
Email: hugo-castro@hotmail.com

ZIMBABWE (Harare)
Networker: Chloe Elkin
PO Box 1623
Harare
Zimbabwe
Tel: 263 91336969
Email: chloeelkin@hotmail.com

How to Start a Network

Appendix 3

From scratch

- Research who is doing what and where. Are they willing to link with others?

- Build relationships by holding a conference or meeting.

- Appoint a link person to encourage growing relationships.

- Use Viva Network for advice and for gaining useful ideas.

Where there is a passive network

- Find a facilitator, someone who will channel information between network members and work on the development of relationships.

- Appoint a steering committee to provide advice and support for the facilitator and to which the network can be accountable.

- Use Viva Network to gain advice on attaining active network status and links to other groups and networks. Also for training of facilitator.

Where there is an active network

- Hold a consultation to appoint a co-ordinator to administer and sustain the network.

- Establish a legally accountable board, where members are elected every one to two years to work towards gaining legal status for the network, to determine the network's affiliations (e.g. to wider networks such as Viva Network), to fundraise, to provide direction and to interface with the wider community on behalf of the network.

- Use Viva Network to gain advice on strategy for proactive network-ing, to link internationally, to gain training and other services pro-vided by Viva Network.

Where there is an active network in partnership with other networks

- Appoint co-ordinators for different areas of concern.

- Ensure board is informed to maintain accountability as a network operates with a variety of partners.

- Use Viva Network for occasional advice to Board and co-ordinator and for introductions to potential new partners.

Why Children? *Appendix 4*

Around a billion people, or one out of every six on the planet, are be-tween 10 and 19 years of age, 85 per cent of them in developing coun-tries.

Source: Geeta Rao Gupta, International Center for Research on Women (ICRW) Progress of the Nations, UNICEF, 1998, p. 21.

AIDS

Worldwide

The World Health Organization estimates that 18 million adults and 1.5 million children have been infected with HIV.

Source: Sue Armstrong and John Williamson, 'Action for Children Affected by AIDS, Programme Profiles and Lessons Learned', WHO/UNICEF Joint Document, 1994.

In 1997 alone, around 3 million young people aged 15 to 24 became infected with HIV, about two-thirds of them girls.

Source: Geeta Rao Gupta, International Center for Research on Women (ICRW) Progress of the Nations, UNICEF, 1998, p. 21.

In 1999, 8.2 million children were living without parents or a mother, due to the spread of AIDS. Estimates for 2000 place the number at 13 million, with 10.4 million of these below the age of 15.

Source: Progress of the Nations, UNICEF, 1999.

Some 15.6 million children had lost their mothers or both of their parents by 2000 in 23 countries heavily affected by HIV/AIDS. That number will increase to 22.9 million by 2010, largely as a result of the HIV/AIDS pandemic.

Source: US Census Bureau via Susan Hunter and John Williamson, 'Children on the Brink: Strategies to Support Children Isolated by HIV/AIDS', United States Agency for International Development, 1997, p. 1.

In Africa

By 2010, orphans will comprise up to 8.9 per cent of children under the age of 15 in sub-Saharan Africa due largely to the spread of HIV/AIDS.

Source: US Census Bureau via Susan Hunter and John Williamson, 'Children on the Brink: Strategies to Support Children Isolated by HIV/AIDS', United States Agency for International Development, 1997, p. 1.

There will be 1,230,000 orphans in Malawi by the end of 1999.

Source: 'Orphan Estimates for 23 Study Countries, 2000' in Susan Hunter and John Williamson, 'Children on the Brink: Strategies to Support Children Isolated by HIV/AIDS', United States Agency for International Development, 1997, figure A-4.

There will be 1,656,000 orphans in Zambia by the end of 1999.

Source: 'Orphan Estimates for 23 Study Countries, 2000' in Susan Hunter and John Williamson, 'Children on the Brink: Strategies to Support Children Isolated by HIV/AIDS', United States Agency for International Development, 1997, figure A-4.

Child labour

Worldwide

An estimated 250 million children work worldwide.

Source: UNICEF, The United Kingdom Committee for UNICEF, 1997–98 Annual Review, p. 6.

Around the globe, 73 million children aged 10 to 14 are working — not counting the tens of millions, mostly girls, believed to be in domestic service.

Source: Geeta Rao Gupta, International Center for Research on Women (ICRW) Progress of the Nations, UNICEF, 1998, p. 21.

In Africa

In Senegal the government estimates that there are between 50,000 and 100,000 children and young people acting as professional street beggars in bondage to Muslim marabouts.

Source: Submission by Anti-Slavery International to United Nations Commission on Human Rights, May 1994.

An estimated 12 million children work in Nigeria.

Source: United Nations Children's Fund — Information Sheet, 29 March 1994.

Some 70 per cent of child leather workers in Egypt work more than eight hours a day, and only half of these attend or plan to attend school.

Source: United Nations Children's Fund — Information Sheet, 29 March 1994.

In Latin America

An estimated 7 million children work in Brazil.

Source: United Nations Children's Fund — Information Sheet, 29 March 1994.

Children of War

Worldwide

More than 1.5 million children have been killed in wars worldwide in the past decade. Over 4 million have been disabled, maimed, blinded and brain damaged, and more than 12 million children have lost their homes in this period.

Source: 'Children at War', Save the Children, 16 November 1994.

Some 35 countries have used child soldiers in the past ten years.

Source: 'Children at War', Save the Children, 16 November 1994.

More than a million children have been orphaned or separated from their peers as a result of war.

Source: 'State of the World's Children' UNICEF report, 1995.

In Africa

During the war in Mozambique at least 8,000 children were forcibly recruited to fight in the Renamo military forces.

Source: British Broadcasting Corporation and Save the Children, 24 October 1994.

The Civilian Defense Forces have reportedly been employing children to fight in Sierra Leone, with one field commander estimating 3,000 in the eastern Kailahun district alone.

Source: Lansana Fofana, 'Militia Admits Recruiting Child Soldiers', IPS, Freetown, Sierra Leone, 29 June 1998.

Child prostitution

Worldwide

Each year a million children are lured or forced into child prostitution.

Source: Norwegian Government Report quoted by Jubilee Action, 1994.

In Southeast Asia

The Centre for the Protection of Children's Rights (CPCR) in Thailand estimates that 80 per cent of girls under 17 who have been rescued from brothels are HIV-positive.

Source: P. Green, 'Prostitution: Children the Victims. The Effects of Prostitution and Sexual Exploitation on Children and Adolescents', unpublished, 1994, p. 4.

In a Thai study of 1,012 adolescents and young adults being prostituted, 90 per cent of respondents disapproved of prostitution and their role in it, 43 per cent felt disappointed in themselves, hopeless and trapped, 50 per cent felt that society showed contempt for them, and 26 per cent stated that they would commit suicide if they knew they had contracted AIDS.

Source: P. Green, 'Prostitution: Children the Victims. The Effects of Prostitution and Sexual Exploitation on Children and Adolescents', unpublished, 1994, p. 3.

Street children

Worldwide

At least 100 million children worldwide are believed to live at least part of the time on the streets and work in the 'urban informal sector' — the fastest-growing area of child labour.

Source: 1998 Information Sheet on Street Children by UNICEF UK Committee, January 1998.

In Asia

There are at least 18 million street children in India.

Source: ONEWORLD, 17 November 1998, cited by UNICEF in November 1998.

In Latin America

There are as many as 40 million street children in Latin America.

Source: ONEWORLD, 17 November 1998, cited by UNICEF in November 1998.

In North America

A survey of 30 US cities found that families with children account for 39 per cent of the homeless population; the same study found that children account for just over a quarter of the homeless population.

Source: Laura Waxman, 'A Status Report on Hunger and Homelessness in America's Cities', 1994, United States Conference of Mayors, 1620 Eye Street, NW 4th Floor, Washington DC 20006.

Bibliography

Maggie Black, 'Children in War', a report, Children's Aid Direct, 1996.

Adrian H. Bredero, Christendom and Christianity in the Middle Ages (Eerdmans, 1994).

Allen D. Clark, A History of the Church in Korea (Christian Literature Society of Korea, 1971).

Linda Dube, 'Surviving in the Streets', paper, July 1998.

David L. Edwards, Christian England, Vol. 3 (Fount, 1984).

Phyllis Kilbourn (ed.), Children in Crisis: A New Commitment (MARC Publications, 1996).

Phyllis Kilbourn, Street Children: A Guide to Effective Ministry (MARC Publications, 1997).

John McManners (ed.), The Oxford Illustrated History of Christianity (Oxford University Press, 1990).

Glenn Myers, Children in Crisis (OM Publishing, 1998).

W.A. Strange, Children in the Early Church (Paternoster Press, 1996).

'The State of the World's Children 1998: Focus on Nutrition' (UNICEF, 1998).

'The State of the World's Children 1999: Education' (UNICEF).

UNICEF Information Sheet, 'All Work and No Play: The scourge of child labour', April 1997.

UNICEF Information Sheet, 'Children in Conflict', undated.

UNICEF Information Sheet, 'Child Prostitution', undated.

Suggestions for Further Reading

Information on the following resources, along with where to obtain them and many others, is to be found in the *Viva Network Directory of Children at Risk Resources*, which contains information about over 500 resources useful to those working with children. It includes public awareness tools, teaching tools for projects, reports on particular countries, and planning aids for specific ministries.

For a full copy of the directory, or to request particular sections, please contact Viva Network or email resourcedirectory@viva.org

General information about children in need

Connect. A magazine published quarterly by Viva Network for people interested in finding out more about children in need. It provides news and informative articles about children in need and Christian work with them.

Streetlife. A creative and stimulating cross-curricular teacher's manual for teaching about street children in secondary schools. This resource contains lesson plans, maps, pictures. Produced by Jubilee Action. Available from Viva Network.

Street Children. This book by Andy Butcher gives a lively introduction to the problem of street children. Hard statistics are combined with stories about individuals. Published by Nelson Word Publishing.

In my own words. A powerful video featuring the stories of three children: a girl from Guatemala, a boy who works as a scavenger in the Philippines and an AIDS orphan from Uganda. A well-produced video to raise awareness of children in need. Available from Compassion International, Colorado, USA.

Children in Crisis. This booklet gives information about child labour, street children, children of war, and children of the sex trade, with suggestions for prayer. Available from D. M. Publishing, Carlisle.

Children in Crisis — A New Commitment. This book edited by Phyllis Kilbourn is a call to missions and churches to face up to the implications of millions of children in crisis around the world. It gives information about the ways in which children are suffering today, and gives biblical reasons for a response. It equips the reader to minister to children in practical ways. This book calls attention to street children, sexual exploitation, AIDS orphans, child labour and war trauma. Published by MARC, World Vision International, 1996.

'Child Labour in Context'. This report by Delia Paul is published by World Vision Australia and seeks to give a balanced perspective on different types of child labour in different areas of the world. It covers child slavery, children in wage labour and self-employed children on the streets. The need to support working children is addressed. Available from World Vision UK, Milton Keynes.

'Working children: Reconsidering the debates'. This thorough but readable report edited by Jim McKechnie and Sandy Hobbs covers the nature of the problem of working children in different regions; the reasons behind the problem of working children; debates about working children; and the role of the IWGCL. It also contains a section in which children's views are given in their own words, and looks at children's role in change. Available from International Working Group on Child Labour, PO Box 75297, 1070 AG Amsterdam.

Projects working with children in need

The Street Children of Brazil. This book by Sarah de Carvalho is the story of how the author left a career in film promotion and TV production to work as a missionary in Brazil with street children. It tells of how Sarah and her husband founded the Child Mission, and relates stories of the children they have met. It is a story of faith, suffering and love. Published by Hodder &Stoughton, London.

Little Outlaws, Dirty Angels: Finding Freedom in the New South Africa. This is Tom Hewitt's inspiring story about his work with street children in South Africa. It explains the situation in South Africa, why children are on the streets and what life is like for them. It describes each stage of work with street children, emphasizing the hope and power of the gospel. This would be a useful book for volunteers interested in short-term work with street children, or those interested in learning more about street children in South Africa. Available from Amos Trust, London.

All God's Children. Mary Batchelor and Ron Newby tell the stories of children in extreme need and their journey to spiritual hope and a life worth living through the work of Christian charity Global Care. Each chapter contains the story of action among a particular group of children in need in a particular country. Information about the country is given, plus photos and stories of children in need and those who work with them. Available from Global Care, Coventry.

Blossoms in the Dust: Street Children in Africa. This book gives a picture of the situation of street children in Africa. Both the stories of individuals and the root of the problem are investigated. The second part of the book evaluates several projects working with street children, and looks at the educational aspects of work with street children in Africa. Available from UNESCO.

Miracle Children: The Toybox Story. This is the autobiography of Duncan Dyason, and a history of the Toybox Charity, which works with street children in Guatemala. Published by Hodder &Stoughton, London.

Working with Street Children. A selection of 18 case studies from Africa, Asia and Latin America, where reinsertion of street children into families and/or society has been effective, with a focus on educational provision. Available from UNESCO.

Practical guides to working with children

Reaching Children at Risk. A practical journal for sharing ideas, information and expertise for those working directly with 'children at risk'. Each issue has articles around a particular theme, such as conflict, education, disability. Available from Viva Network.

Crisis on the streets...A manual for ministry to street children. This practical handbook includes sections on the world scenario with regard to street children, biblical foundations for work, becoming an effective street worker, getting started in ministry (vision, research, development, accountability), networking, confronting drug issues. The author, Jeff Anderson, works with street children in the Philippines. Available from Action International UK.

Street and working children — a guide to planning. Save the Children Development Manual number 4 gives practical advice for anyone interested in starting or improving a ministry to street and working children. Includes chapters on understanding the children, accessing available information, conducting your own research, different types of projects, managing human resources. It is a stimulating resource, providing ideas and examples of methods that have worked elsewhere. Available from Save the Children, London.

Street Children: Resource Sheets for Project Management. This pack of materials contains information sheets on understanding street children, offering a range of services, day centres and shelters, working with families and communities, advocacy, setting up and organization, project planning, financial management. Available from Childhope UK, London.

Jobs for Life: A manual for ministry in vocational training for children at risk. This manual is produced by Viva Network. It provides information and advice to those who are considering starting a new ministry, as well as project leaders looking to improve their practice. The manual seeks to emphasize practical issues, and is based on an analysis of four projects.

Helping Children in Difficult Circumstances — A Teacher's Manual. A guide book by Naomi Richardson on how to support children who have been affected by their experiences of violence, with special emphasis on the role of teachers. Available from Save the Children.

Helping Children Cope with the Stresses of War — A Manual for Parents and Teachers. This book by Mona Macksoud is based on methods and approaches that have been tested extensively in Lebanon and Kuwait. It contains general guidelines for teachers and parents on handling the 'problem behaviours' with which children respond to stresses, giving concrete practical advice. Available from UNICEF.

Working with Traumatized Children: A Guide for Teachers and Caregivers. Written by Oasis Counselling Centre, Nairobi, following the bomb explosion in August 1998 to help teachers counselling children. This book is also more widely applicable to helping traumatized children. It covers emotional reactions in children, helping children cope with loss, ideas for activities, and how to explain to children what has happened. Available from Viva Network.

Children and Trauma: Fostering Healing and Supporting Recovery. Workshop notes for those who work with children who have experienced trauma. Contains 30 pages of practical guidelines. Available from World Vision UK.

Street Children — A Guide to Effective Ministry. This handbook edited by Phyllis Kilbourn is designed to motivate and equip workers among street children. Examples are given from every continent and many cities to explain who street children are, where they are found, why they are on the streets and the nature of their trauma. The handbook gives a profile of the street worker, examines bonding issues, explains the cycle of addiction to the streets, and more. Published by MARC, World Vision International, 1997. Also available from WEC International.

Sexually Exploited Children: Working to Protect and Heal. Edited by Phyllis Kilbourn and Marjorie McDermid, this practical resource helps you to become an effective instrument to facilitate Christ's healing and love to broken children. Published by MARC, World Vision International, 1998. Available from WEC International.

Healing the Children of War — A Handbook for Ministry to Children Who Have Suffered Deep Traumas. This book edited by Phyllis Kilbourn gives in-depth practical guidance to Christians who desire to be of service to children whose lives have been shattered by conflict or other trauma. The chapters cover the impact of war upon children, understanding troubled children, listening to the child, play therapy, conflict resolution, forgiveness, and restoration of hope. Published by MARC, World Vision International, 1995. Available from WEC International.

God's Heart for the Poor. Philippa Stroud (with Christine Leonard) has written an excellent little book on how to run a long-term care project based on a local church. Available from Kingsway Publications.